W9-BDQ-090

GUIDE TO
FICTION WRITING

BOOKS BY PHYLLIS A. WHITNEY

Adult Novels

FLAMING TREE
DREAM OF ORCHIDS
VERMILION
POINCIANA
DOMINO
THE GLASS FLAME
THE STONE BULL
THE GOLDEN UNICORN
SPINDRIFT
THE TURQUOISE MASK
SNOWFIRE
LISTEN FOR THE WHISPERER
LOST ISLAND
THE WINTER PEOPLE
HUNTER'S GREEN
RAINSONG

EMERALD
SILVERHILL
COLUMBELLA
SEA JADE
BLACK AMBER
SEVEN TEARS FOR APOLLO
WINDOW ON THE SQUARE
BLUE FIRE
THUNDER HEIGHTS
THE MOONFLOWER
SKYE CAMERON
THE TREMBLING HILLS
THE QUICKSILVER POOL
THE RED CARNELIAN
SILVERSWORD
FEATHER ON THE MOON

Novels for Young People

NOBODY LIKES TRINA
CREOLE HOLIDAY
THE FIRE AND THE GOLD
THE HIGHEST DREAM
A LONG TIME COMING
STEP TO THE MUSIC
LOVE ME, LOVE ME NOT

LINDA'S HOMECOMING
EVER AFTER
WILLOW HILL
THE SILVER INKWELL
A WINDOW FOR JULIE
A STAR FOR GINNY
A PLACE FOR ANN

Mysteries for Young People

SECRET OF THE STONE FACE
SECRET OF HAUNTED MESA
MYSTERY OF THE SCOWLING BOY
THE VANISHING SCARECROW
SECRET OF THE MISSING
  FOOTPRINT
MYSTERY OF THE CRIMSON
  GHOST
SECRET OF GOBLIN GLEN
SECRET OF THE SPOTTED SHELL
MYSTERY OF THE ANGRY IDOL
SECRET OF THE EMERALD STAR

MYSTERY OF THE HIDDEN HAND
MYSTERY OF THE GOLDEN HORN
SECRET OF THE TIGER'S EYE
MYSTERY OF THE HAUNTED
  POOL
SECRET OF THE SAMURAI SWORD
MYSTERY OF THE GREEN CAT
MYSTERY ON THE ISLE OF SKYE
MYSTERY OF THE BLACK
  DIAMONDS
MYSTERY OF THE STRANGE
  TRAVELER

MYSTERY OF THE GULLS

Textbooks

GUIDE TO FICTION WRITING
WRITING JUVENILE STORIES AND NOVELS

G U I D E T O
FICTION WRITING

PHYLLIS A. WHITNEY

THE WRITER, INC.
PUBLISHERS   BOSTON

Manufactured in the United States of America

Quality Printing and Binding by:
R R. Donnelley & Sons Company
1009 Sloan Street
Crawfordsville, IN 47933 U.S.A.

0-87116-157-5

CONTENTS

INTRODUCTION

Joanne Greenberg (author of *I Never Promised You a Rose Garden*) has said that writers can be divided into two categories: those who are "venturesome" and those who are "consistent." She suggests that the venturesome writer has more fun, while the consistent writer is likely to attain greater success.

Perhaps our temperaments give us little choice in the matter, yet it seems to me that compromise is possible and that we can have a great deal of fun writing within certain chosen limitations. By this time I am certainly a consistent writer. Having found my niche, I've worked out a pattern that enables me to venture within its broad boundaries and never find myself bored.

When we start out as writers we *need* to explore our own talents. We can't possibly know where we will write most comfortably until we've followed various leads. We may not even be sure whether we are fiction or nonfiction writers. I have known successful nonfiction writers who long to write fiction but somehow lack the flair. Perhaps one of the answers to satisfaction in any creative work is to accept our own limitations, whatever they are, while still continuing to hone our skills so we can push out those limits for as long as we write. In the end, of course, we need compete only with ourselves.

Ever since I was about twelve, I have wanted—not to *be* a writer—but to *write.* I loved to make up stories and set them down on paper. When I was teaching writing, it always surprised me to discover how many beginners saw their goal only as becoming famous and earning a lot of money. These were the ones who fell by the wayside, since they weren't willing to work at becoming a writer. For a great many years, even after I had grown up, my stories were pretty bad. I didn't realize then that it was supposed to be that way, that of course I would not be a good writer until I'd practiced for a long time and learned how to use the tools of my craft.

Only a handful of writers and artists start out by creating masterpieces, and in some ways they are to be pitied because their success is accidental and they have no idea how it came about. For them, everything fell into place by chance, and they are unable to repeat their success without serving an apprenticeship; harder to do after a too easy taste of success. Perhaps stumbling through a period of poor writing and all too many rejection slips is a surer way of mastering one's craft.

For a number of years I didn't know that I wasn't a short story writer. I'd written about three hundred short stories, only a hundred of which had sold. Every story was a struggle to write, and my imagination wouldn't create new ideas quickly enough. Not until I found that I needed the book length to move around in did I begin to be happier as a writer. However, even after I wrote my first book, a teenage novel, I still didn't know where I belonged. I ventured through periods of writing career novels for girls, teenage problem novels, period novels, mysteries for early teens—each time becoming tired of what I was doing and always searching for new territory. I was being published and I was earning a modest living. But I wasn't satisfied.

I was afraid to try the adult market. I'd listened to too many "critics" who thought I wasn't "good enough," forgetting that writing for young people is perhaps more difficult than writing for adults. Reading Daphne du Maurier's *Rebecca* freed me; it gave me a feeling of excitement that I thought I might be able to capture in my own writing. I'd always loved mysteries, though not detective stories, and luckily for me there was a wider group of readers for romantic suspense than for most detective novels.

So—I wrote *The Quicksilver Pool* as my first effort in this field. It was my nineteenth book. The other eighteen were published juveniles, one adult murder mystery (which sold very few copies), and one how-to book on juvenile writing. My "pool" cast hardly a ripple, but I liked what I was doing, and I wrote more novels in this genre. Paperback publishers would have none of me at first. *(Who would read that sort of book?)* It was years before they "discovered" me. But I was writing the kind of book I enjoyed and that challenged me to persist in that type of writing without growing stale or bored.

I found that I could keep my own interest alive by using a new setting for each novel, and I could research fresh subjects that would open worlds to me that I'd previously known nothing about. Now I could be both *venturesome* and *consistent*—a good combination for attracting readers.

Through all this searching and experimenting, one common denominator has become clear to me: I was learning how to tell a good story. Through my own experiences as a writer, and through the teaching of writing, I began to understand the basics of storytelling. This is the one element in fiction writing that can be taught. No one can give you the drive to write. No one can give you the special talent you'll need. But talent can be developed from its early raw state and helped to grow. We need never be afraid of so-called rules. They aren't set in concrete, but are only guidelines. Once you understand how to hold and interest a reader, how to build a sound plot, you can push out in any direction. When someone tells me I can't do something, I say to myself, "Let's see how I can get around this stumbling block effectively." I can manage this only because by now I know how the rules work.

These guidelines are what I have set down in this book. Many young writers (and older writers who are also beginners) have written to tell me that this approach has helped them to attain publication. Such letters are my special reward. I have been there, and I know how rejection feels. I like success a great deal better, but I've had to earn it. And so must you.

Phyllis A. Whitney

GUIDE TO
FICTION WRITING

PART ONE
METHODS AND PROCESS

1

OPPORTUNITY IS LIKE A TRAIN

I hadn't seen my friend for many years when we came face to face that day at Kennedy Airport. I had known her in Chicago when we were both young and belonged to the same small writing group. I can remember that I'd been a little in awe of her then because she wrote so well and two of her stories had appeared in slick-paper magazines—the goal of most young writers in those days. My own market was the "pulps," and I had been afraid I wasn't ever going to be good enough for anything else. I'd had a hard time living through all the rejection slips until I could be published in the lowliest of markets. But now, when I met this former friend again, I was "successful."

Though we were taking different planes that day, we had time between planes to exchange reminiscences, and I asked about her writing. She shrugged and said, "I've been busy with other things. There's never enough time, so I'm not writing anymore. I never had your luck anyway."

Later I thought about that quite soberly, and perhaps with more than a touch of irritation. This wasn't the first time I had been told I was lucky—with my books turning up on bestseller lists in both hard and softcover, becoming book club selections, being published abroad. Sometimes I sensed a faint envy behind the accusation, even a reproach. My talent in the beginning had certainly been modest, and these writers knew it. They didn't make the distinction that it had been an untrained talent, and that I'd learned how to harness and train it. They only knew that I hadn't been as gifted as they felt they were. So why had I been successful, when they were not?

Of course, I have been lucky. I've had extraordinary breaks come my way—along with some pretty bad blows and disappointments. There's been bad luck too, but that doesn't always show. Good fortune and unexpected opportunities are always coming along. Perhaps opportunity is like a train on an endless track. Now and then it makes a stop at your station, often without fanfare, and without warning.

I remember a stop that train made when I was still living in Chicago and had published my first three books—teenage novels. One day a successful older writer phoned me and said, "I've recommended you to the editor of the new book section for the *Chicago Sun* [now the *Sun-Times*]. He's looking for a reviewer of children's books, and since you've written in that field, go down to see him if you're interested."

My first impulse was to panic. Why would he want *me*? I lacked a "name," and I knew nothing at all about book reviewing. But I went downtown to his office and talked to him for a few minutes. He didn't promise anything, though he said I could try writing a few reviews for him. I came home with three very different juvenile books under my arm, and the feeling that I was biting off something I didn't know how to chew. He had told me he was trying out a number of people in order to find a reviewer who suited him.

I wrote the reviews. I got the job. How very, very lucky that the train had stopped where I could get aboard. Or was it possible that without realizing it I had been getting ready for that train for a long time?

During those years when I had been writing without getting published, then with a little very modest success in magazines, and finally having some books published, I had worked hard to learn my craft. I had read widely in the juvenile field, and I'd studied books and articles on writing. *Because* I'd been learning something about my craft, I could read the books assigned me for review and understand what was good and what was bad about them. And as a fiction writer, I knew I had to be interesting and lively in *whatever* I wrote. So I was ready when the train stopped—and my future life took a turn for the better. Any number of "lucky breaks" arose from my work as a reviewer. Of course I didn't change direction from the main road of my life, which was to write more books of fiction. Whatever extras I did after that were always fitted into the afternoon hours. Or evenings. My mornings have always been for my "real" writing.

What is important is not the lucky break, the stopping of the train—that's only part of it. Life is full of trains that stop. What counts is what we are doing with our lives when there *is no opportunity* and not a train in sight.

My life has been full of such opportunities, and looking back I have found that the lucky breaks that worked out were *generally followed or preceded by some positive action on my part.* Two in particular are significant.

After a number of years, I had published quite a few titles in the juvenile field, and my name was beginning to be recognized to some degree. Nevertheless, I couldn't earn a living by my writing alone, and I was reviewing and lecturing and teaching writing at New York University. Then the inevitable happened, and I found myself going stale. I was getting very tired of teen-age love. And because I was losing interest, my last teen-age novel hadn't been very good. I tried to write some adult short stories, but they all flopped. I really wasn't a short story writer and didn't like the constriction of the short form.

Then one day I learned that a man I'd known in a writing group in Chicago had recently become manager of a new book club. I went to his Manhattan office to congratulate him and talk a little about old times. He took me to lunch, and I confessed that I was bored with what I was writing and had the feeling that I needed a change. He told me that his book club was looking for entertaining novels for women, which would be both romantic and suspenseful. "We want the kind of love stories you used to do for the pulps, but more adult, better written, and with strong characterization. I think you could do it. If you want to try an adult novel that might interest us, we'll find a publisher for you if we like it."

I went home enormously excited, with renewed enthusiasm, and took stock: I liked to *read* romantic novels with a touch of suspense and mystery. One of my recent short story rejects had these elements, and perhaps I could write a novel using that story idea. Furthermore, it seemed to me that the kind of novel the book club was looking for could use especially interesting and unusual backgrounds—one of the things I had featured in all my previous writing. I was living on Staten Island, and it occurred to me that what had happened there during the Civil War was fascinating and would make a good background for the novel I would try to write.

The book that resulted from that "lucky break" was *The Quicksilver Pool.* My friend at the book club and his fiction editor liked it and suggested several publishers. But first I wanted to try it out with my own publishers, who had brought out my juveniles. Three editors in the adult departments of these publishers turned down the new effort. Sometimes what seems like disaster when it happens, proves to be good luck in the long run. What resulted changed my life once more and pointed in the direction I've taken. I next turned to the publishers who my book club friend thought would be interested. I selected Appleton-Century-Crofts. The woman who became my editor there has worked with me on every romantic suspense novel I've published since, and she later became my agent.

The books I wrote for Appleton, however, made no great splash, though my editor believed in them. The book club readers were pleased—which meant a somewhat larger income and audience for me, and each of my following novels was selected for as long as the book club lasted. I alternated between writing romantic suspense novels for adults and mystery books for ten-to-fourteen-year-olds. (No more teen-age love!) My income wasn't large, but I was happy doing what I liked to do, and I was learning how to do it better.

At that time the paperback publishers wouldn't touch my books. The men editors of softcover books said there was no market for the sort of thing I was writing, so not one of my romantic suspense novels was brought out in paper. I kept right on doing what I wanted to do, and suddenly the train stopped again—without my even knowing it, without my having to do anything more than I was already doing. One of the paperback editors noticed that his mother's favorite novel was *Rebecca*, by Daphne du Maurier. He was thinking of trying a series of such books for women readers, and he cast around for possible titles. The first one he decided to publish was my *Thunder Heights*. The publisher called the new series "Gothics," and the run was on. It wasn't that other such books weren't already being published here and there, and even in paper by one perceptive woman editor, but until that moment no one had pulled them together and given them a "category" label. Now there was a "band-wagon"—and I was aboard.

My books began to sell in paper and were picked up and published abroad. Magazines here and in other countries began to publish me serially and in con-densed versions. I had backed into the slick magazine markets that I had never been able to reach with short stories.

When the breaks came for me I was doing the right thing. I didn't know it was the right thing, but even when there was no opportunity in sight, I was working. You, who may be just beginning: What you do *now* counts. Never mind the rejections, the discouragement, the voices of ridicule (there can be those too). Work and wait and learn, and that train will come by. If you give up, you'll never have a chance to climb aboard.

2

WORKING HABITS

As a writer, you are your own boss, and working discipline is the most important habit of all to develop.

Every beginning writer, and sometimes the experienced one, suffers from the temptation *not* to write. You'll undoubtedly find certain enticements to lure you away from your typewriter. The mail must be read—always a dangerous distraction, because then there are letters you must answer immediately. Pencils must be sharpened, that telephone call must be made, and of course that shopping you need to do is very important. Would it matter if you take the morning off? Yes, it *would* matter!

Or perhaps you just don't feel like writing today. This is the best—and worst—excuse of all, and unless you are too ill to get out of bed, you should pay no attention to it. By now my own working habits are stronger than any of the distractions, though I am not a tense, driven workaholic. When my writing period is behind me, I can set my writing aside to do other things. But being a moderate workaholic can make your life very interesting and worthwhile. You'll never have to fill your time with make-believe enterprises.

The first important step is to choose a stretch of time that you can spend regularly on writing—an hour, or three hours a day, weekends or evenings, if you have a full-time job. Find a period that is comfortable and possible for you. Some people, like me, are morning people; others do their best work at night.

You will need to be firm if you have a family. You'll need to make others understand that this *Writing Time* is sacred and not to be interrupted. In the beginning they'll feel that you have no right to sequester yourself. Who do you think you are—a writer? So you say to yourself and to others, "Yes, I *am* a writer. I write, and I am a writer." Of course nobody believes this in the beginning. But you stick to your typewriter and your schedule, and one day—to the astonishment of all—you place a published story, a published book, before their disbelieving eyes. Only then will those around you begin to understand that you really do need time to be alone and write.

No matter how many books you publish, this is a battle you'll have to fight all your life. You'll need to tell your friends not to call you at certain hours, and if they are friends, they will comply, however puzzled. You'll give up invitations you might like to accept, and miss out on all sorts of occasions and activities.

Men writers who are married to non-working wives —that is, wives who stay at home—have a certain advantage. Every writer needs a wife!—someone to stand guard, to cook meals, to deal with the immediate problems of house and children, and keep them out of their husbands' hair. It's more difficult for women writers, who have to do all these chores *plus* their writing.

When a man (or a woman) writer works at an outside job, it is equally rough. In the beginning, outside jobs are usually necessary. Nevertheless, we all write somehow—*making time*—and habit grows strong with practice. The challenge is always the same: How *much* do you want to write? Not just to be a writer, but *to write*.

Once the time problem is worked out, however unsatisfactorily in the beginning, you must develop your own writing pattern. You will need to overcome your self-consciousness about that sheet of paper with nothing on it. You *are* going to fill it. When you do, then at the end of your hour, or whatever time you have, you'll feel pleased with yourself and everything else all day long.

Once you have something down on paper, you'll have an easier time getting back to work the next day. You read through what you've written, making corrections, or you do it over. Your imagination catches fire, and you move ahead with new writing. Or if you have trouble pushing on, the material in your notebook can be worked on, so that you always have something you can do to renew the creative flow. I'll tell you about my notebook plan in the next chapter. It can become an important part of your working habits.

There is certainly such a thing as an "itch to write." I have it all the time now, and I know I had it even in the beginning, when I really didn't know what to do about it, or how to set a finished story down on paper. If you're a writer, that "itch" will come to your aid, and it can be constructively trained.

Another unhappy truth that you might as well accept from the start is that *life* will never leave you alone. The demands of daily living will cut into your time, insist on your attention, shake you up badly, or sometimes even so delight you that you can't concentrate on writing. Or so you think. But you'll learn to use what comes, good and bad, and it will become part of whatever you are, and find its way under many disguises into your work. Some writers don't feel they have really lived an experience, however joyful or sorrowful, until they have written about it. There are even times when it becomes our escape into an imaginary country where we can ease our minds from all that is troubling. When we come back to the "real" world, we feel renewed and better able to cope with whatever problems beset us.

An important aspect of your work discipline is to develop the habit of observation and analysis—of yourself and others. What do you make of what is happening to you and around you? I have never cared to keep a diary about everyday factual happenings, but now and then I enter what I think about something in a sort of off-and-on journal. Oddly enough, when I am happy and contented and busy, I seldom go near that journal. But when things go wrong, I find that it helps to work them out a bit on paper—even before they become part of my story writing.

Of course you type. Well, if you don't, then learn as quickly as possible. Too much time can be lost if you try to write everything by hand. This was my problem as a very young writer. So I bought a book on typing and took a couple of weeks to work at the drills every day until I could compose on the machine. I still pick up my pencil for thinking purposes, before I get down to the actual writing. And sometimes I do whole revision scenes in pencil right on the back of a manuscript page. These days I can go very fast on the keys. I can make mistakes faster than almost anyone! Which doesn't matter, since I don't have to be perfect. An editor will read a neatly corrected manuscript—though not one filled with insertions. Nowadays, I have my final copy professionally typed.

People are always commenting on how well organized I am. I'm sure this is true in many ways. But I have only to look at the piles of paper on my desk, and wonder. Because there is never enough time for everything—but after all, isn't that the best way to live?

By now, my working habits—the ones that count most to me as a writer—are firmly entrenched, and I no longer have to push myself to get to work. I enjoy being my own boss. My office is wherever I choose to have it, and my time is my own to do with as I please. As it happens, I please to write. But I had to earn that privilege.

What I like best of all are those working hours when something magical comes to life and I can create something as real as a book, when there was nothing at all when I started.

3

PLANNING YOUR NOVEL
The Notebook:
Preliminaries

One of the benefits I derived from twelve years of teaching the craft of writing, was the development of a working method so valuable to me that I was able to step up my output and improve the quality of my writing as well. This method has proved useful not only to me, but to others—former writing students and those who have read my articles and have written to tell me how well my system has worked for them.

There is nothing very startling or original about it; mostly it's an application of common sense to the organization of your work. While this method has been well tested, and I have great confidence in it *for me,* it certainly is not the only way to write a novel. It may not be the best way for you. As you write, you must arrange your periods of planning, writing, and revision to suit yourself.

Perhaps you're one of those lucky writers who can plunge in, write at high speed with little preparation, with ideas coming to you as you write. There are many successful writers who work in exactly that way—though sometimes I think these writers "find" their "outline" by writing through to the end. And often they must do another quite different draft later on.

Whatever means you use to finish a novel must feel right for *you*. I only know that when I began to write I had difficulty keeping my interest high after the first few chapters. My ideas fizzled out rather quickly because I didn't know in advance where I was going. There were frightening "dry spells" when nothing moved. I learned how painful it could be to *want* to write, and yet find myself unable to fill those blank pages—sometimes for weeks on end. I needed to find a way to keep my story growing so that I would never run dry.

Before I developed my present working methods, I used to keep a folder in which I dropped odds and ends of characterization, bits of narrative, stray story ideas, as they occurred to me. There was never enough of anything, and it was never organized for easy finding.

Not until I began to teach an evening writing class at a university did I come to grips with my own problem. In order to tell students anything useful about the writing of a full-length novel, I'd have to work out a more sensible system for myself first—one I could then present to others.

I began with a simple organization of my time and my material. I gave up the idea that I must always spend my three hours a day in creative work at my typewriter. As the system developed, I found that do-

ing much more preparatory work than I'd been willing to spend before was paying off and shortening my
efforts in the long run. Being able to keep constructively busy on some phase of my notebook, whether I
was actually writing or not, was wonderfully stimulating to my imagination, and it kept the creative flow
high.

The method, roughly, is to give as much time as I
need to the planning phase—developing characters
and plot, collecting all the stray ideas that may be
useful, doing a sketchy outline, working back and
forth in my notebook until a rich fund of material
begins to emerge. The real heart of my notebook system has to do with Plotting, Characters, and Outline,
and I will deal with these in detail in the next chapter.
Once I have worked through all these notebook sections and can start writing—I *go!*

I recognize that most young writers are impatient to
write and can't wait to begin. That's the way it was
with me, and if you succeed, fine. That will be your
way. However, if you run into trouble along the road,
you may be able to adapt the method I use to whatever phase of writing you're in.

My rough breakdown of time runs something like
this: Two months for the planning; four months for the
writing; two months to do it over. Of course, that
timetable seldom works out exactly that way. The
planning may go so fast that I'm through in a month or
less. The writing may take a shorter time, or longer
than I expect. And the revision may go on for the rest
of the year on some novels, and require very little
time for others.

One of the questions most often asked of me is:
"How long does it take to write a novel?" My answer is

always the same: "It takes as long as it takes." Every book is different, just as you will be a different person at different times in your writing life. Don't feel that you must pin yourself down to a rigid schedule. Let your material and your own inclination guide you. After you are published, of course, there may be deadlines and certain demands that will move in on you from outside and force you to comply.

Although the heart of my notebook covers plotting, characters, and outline, there are important preliminaries that I follow. My notebook is a looseleaf binder with *large rings* that will hold a thick stack of paper. I prefer unlined paper, $5^{1}/2'' \times 7^{1}/2''$, a size that is easier to handle than bigger sheets. I like loose leaves because they can be taken out and spread on my desk, and yet can be put back in place where I'll find them again quickly.

My notebook is divided into sections and labeled with gummed tabs. This labeling is an arbitrary matter, and even the order of the sections is arbitrary. You may want to arrange yours to suit yourself—or to suit the particular novel you are working on. You should be relaxed and flexible about any plan and tailor it to your needs and pattern.

Sometimes I discard headings that I've grown away from. Or I insert new ones as I find I need them for a new novel. Probably most professional writers develop some sort of system for themselves, but the novice who is writing a first novel may not know where to begin, and these suggestions may help. I'll explain each divison of my notebook in order.

CALENDAR

Calendar is my first section, and the first page is headed *Work Calendar.* Under it I enter the date when I start work on a current novel. Later, I enter the title of the book when I know it. Near the top of this first page I write: *Plotting Begun, Plotting Finished,* with spaces for entering dates. Sometimes when I feel that I've been working on a book forever, I can go back and check the actual date. Or if I find that I'm moving too slowly, these dates serve to remind me to stop wasting time. I will also want a record of when I started the writing, when I finished the revision, and how long the final typing took, and when I put the manuscript into the mail.

Finally, I write a rough estimate of length as a guide. Perhaps: 20 chapters, 15 pages each = 300 pages.

You may want to set down some figures here to guide you as to total length. Otherwise, you may run on too long and write too many words for the current market. That is, it helps to set down an approximate length for your chapters, and an overall page length for your book. You may not follow this exactly, but some guidelines will restrain you, keep you within bounds.

Under these last notations, which run across the page and use up only a portion of it, I draw a horizontal line, to show a new division, and divide the remaining space vertically into two equal columns. When I'm ready to start writing, I note the month as a heading in the left-hand column, and under it, the date and day of the week. Opposite these, in the same column, I note the number of the manuscript page I reach on that day, and the total wordage to date: Mon., 12—p. 26— 6500 words. (This isn't the amount I wrote on that day, but my total to date.)

Before I'm through, both columns will be filled with this data, and I will probably need to rule another page.

I try to hold myself to six days of writing a week (about three hours at a stretch, which seems right for me, but may be totally wrong for you), with a blank line drawn opposite my one day off, Sunday. On days when no pages are written, I set down the reason: "Plotting ahead," "Revising," or whatever the reason is. Only occasionally do I have to admit that I've done no work at all.

This page is intended for one purpose: to keep me at my desk, at my work. It is so easy to say, "I don't feel like writing today." But I know that will leave an accusing gap in my record, and such gaps add up to not getting a novel done on schedule. Besides, if there are too many days when we don't feel like writing, we'd better examine what we're doing and find out the cause.

TITLES

Here I note any and all ideas for a title as they come to me. I like best to find my title before I even start writing. It's wonderful when one springs into your mind and you can fit it into your story from the beginning. Sometimes a title may even lead you to your plot. My *Mystery of the Green Cat*—a book for young people—was such a title. It popped into my mind as intriguing, but I didn't know what the green cat could possibly be until I got into the planning stage.

Unfortunately, there are other times when I may have a book nearly finished before I can come up with the right title, after a great deal of struggle and much discarding of those that won't work. All these trial flights are recorded in this section, and sometimes a title that isn't right will give me a word I can use for a better title. So I keep track.

For the most part, the titles I choose are the ones that are used on my published novel. I prefer the concrete to the abstract, because it's easier to remember. Many of my books use an object in the title. I seem to have leaned hard on metals, precious stones, and colors, but these seem always to fit into the story and be useful to me. *Sea Jade* worked on several scores: There was jade from the Orient and also a seafaring heritage. *Sea Jade* became the name of the ship in the story, and there might even be a play on the word "jade," in its old usage.

My strangest adventure in finding a title bears repeating because it has to do with the curious workings of the writer's unconscious. I was writing about the red rock country of Sedona, Arizona, and was still struggling for a title by the time three-quarters of the book was written. From my thesaurus, when everything else had failed, I copied down all the interesting words for "red" that I could find. Nothing worked. Finally, in despair, I sent in a list that included *The Vermilion Cliffs*. I didn't like it—there have been too many "cliff" stories, and it sounded corny. But it was suggested that I think of *Vermilion* alone as a title: "Could someone in the story be named Vermilion?"

I instantly rejected this. Of course not! How could

anyone be named Vermilion? Besides, it was the wrong color for those red rocks of Sedona. Feeling distracted and unable to work, I dropped everything and went for a walk, repeating that tantalizing word over and over in my mind. And suddenly I had the whole thing! There *would* be a very strange character called Vermilion, though I would have to write her in all the way through and give the reason behind her existence and her name. Very little else had to be changed because she seemed to belong, and there were places for her to come in. She gave the whole book a strength and mysterious character that it had lacked before.

Occasionally, I dip into *Bartlett's Quotations,* looking up subjects that might lead me to a title. *A Long Time Coming* is taken from a Carl Sandburg poem and fits the story of intolerance toward migrant workers. Another quotation from Civil War writings gave me *Step to the Music.* The first title is too abstract and hard to remember; the second more dramatic and appealing.

Titles deserve thought and care. They form your first means of capturing the attention of an editor, and later must appeal to librarians, booksellers, reviewers —and last, but far from least, the readers who may pick up your book because the title makes them curious.

On days when nothing else about your story will stir, you can turn to your page of titles and ponder awhile; see if you can coax a few titles into being, one of which may be useful to you.

CHRONOLOGY

This section has two divisions—simply because neither one takes much space. The first is headed *Chapters,* and when I start writing, I put down the Roman
numeral of the chapter on the left, leave a space across
the page, and enter near the right-hand margin the
number of my manuscript page on which that chapter
begins. When the chapter is written, I put in paren-
theses the number of pages it covers. You can quickly
lose control of chapter lengths and forget where you
are, unless you keep a record. If you want to change
your chapter lengths later, this record will serve as a
guide.

The second division under the heading of *Chronol-
ogy* deals with information about characters and story
events. How old was this person at this particular
time? Will he or she be the right age to play the role
you require? This becomes particularly important
when there are several generations in the story. How
old is the grandmother of your twenty-six-year-old
heroine? Knowing such details, whether you reveal
them in the novel or not, will help you be consistent.
You'd be surprised at how many small mistakes an
author can make that will also slip by editors and copy
readers, only to be pounced upon by the readers.

If there are major historic events going on at the
time your novel takes place, you will need to make
sure the dates are noted accurately and your story
events parallel them, if they are important. In writing
a novel you must juggle so many details at once that
you can't possibly remember them all, and you will

find it convenient to look them up quickly in your notebook.

THEME, SITUATION

Again, two divisions are combined. The first— *Theme*— deals with the ultimate meaning you want to convey in your novel. It is the point you make at the end. Probably it will deal with whatever you want your characters to learn. If the main character doesn't change—either grow or deteriorate—you have no story. Story significance is discussed elsewhere in this book, so I will only touch on it here.

As early as you can in the planning stage, set down your theme in simple words. Then try to think of the arguments for and against it. Sometimes you won't be sure of the final meaning that you want to point up until much later in the writing of your book. It helps, however, to set down all the guidelines and "clues," all the supporting ideas as they come to you. When you are at a sticking point, you may find it useful to pick up a pencil and casually make notes about your story's meaning. Then later, as you write, you will find yourself picking up some of these points, and it will help if you can turn back and read what you've set down about them.

The second division in this section is *Situation*. I've put it in with theme, not because there's any connection, but to save space. (I told you it was arbitrary.)

The first writing you do in your notebook may be to elaborate on the basic story situation that you have in mind. You may have been collecting some vague ideas, a character or two, a problem, an ending—anything at all. Write any of this under *Situation,* in whatever detail comes to you. For me, the basic situation is usually a character faced by a problem to be set against a background I've already chosen. While I am working on one novel, ideas for another one may come to me, and I enter whatever I have under *Situation* in order not to lose track of such ideas.

Situation material is what you start out with, but once it is down, you probably won't add to it at that point in your notebook. The rest of your notebook will be an elaboration of this opening situation and will be broken into separate phases of your growing novel.

4

A MAP IS NOT A JOURNEY
The Heart of the Matter

In the previous chapter I've been dealing with scheduling and various preparations for writing, all of which have a place in your early planning. Now we get down to the major divisions of the notebook.

PLOTTING

The pages in this main section will keep growing long after you're into the writing of your novel. Good ideas may come to you at any time, no matter how much of the novel is written, and you keep adding to them here.

The items you include in this section needn't be connected to each other at the start. Later on, the connections may become apparent, and you can become selective, discarding what you may never use. I follow a free-association method just to get everything down as it comes to mind, and so I won't lose a thought that may seem clear at the time, but can (and often does) disappear from memory by tomorrow.

I like to do most of my "idle" thinking with a pencil, even though I'll eventually compose on the typewriter. Sometimes an idea that I set down under *Plotting* can run for a page or more. Others are no more than a sentence or two. As they are ultimately incorporated into the *Outline,* or written into the story, I cross them out to cut down on bulk. For me, this *Plotting* section may run 40 to 70 pages, or even more, depending on how rich a vein of inventiveness I'm mining. The whole purpose is to keep your story ideas "developing" as painlessly as possible.

As this section grows, you may want to index it so that you can quickly locate any item or idea that you need at the moment. You'll read through these notes again and again, whenever you're stumped for new directions for your plot, or are searching for new complications, or find that your writing isn't moving ahead. Number the pages and items so you can index them if you wish. This indexing is for convenience and needn't be elaborate or formal. Select headings that are most useful to you. This is only intended to help locate a specific idea that you may have entered earlier and now want to find.

CHARACTERS

Early in planning my story—in fact, as soon as I have something down under *Situation,* I begin to test names for my characters, noting these on a separate page, and trying out various combinations. Often I rename the characters several times, if the names I choose first don't seem to fit as the characters grow. You'll find that a character will know when a name is right, and will accept it comfortably.

At this point I do something fairly mechanical. I set down in two columns the first letter of the first name, and the first letter of each last name of all my characters. I consult this growing list of initials as I name my characters, in order to avoid writing a whole novel before discovering that I've used too many names beginning with the same letter. Sam and Sara and Susan, for instance, or Johnson, Jamison, and Jones. If you watch in your fiction reading, you'll discover this curious first-letter obsession operating with a great many writers who ought to know better. It can become annoying to the reader.

I slipped up when it came to Leigh and Laura in *Listen for the Whisperer,* and by the time I realized they could be easily confused, it was too late to make a change. Once a character becomes firmly attached to the name you've chosen, it becomes an integral part of the characterization and will be almost impossible to change. I can't tell you why this should be so, but any writer who has encountered the obstinacy of an imaginary character will recognize what I mean. So be careful about those names.

Once I have my cast complete, I write a separate character sketch for each that can run for as long as I have anything to say to myself about the people in my story. Spending time on your characters and really getting to know them will pay off.

As you describe each character in turn, setting

down not only outward characteristics, but what goes on in their minds, you'll find that new plotting ideas will come to you, and you will move back and forth between the *Plotting* and *Characters* sections of your notebook. Don't list mere traits or types, but discuss in detail your characters' likes and dislikes, and try to understand how they come to be. Set down anything that will help bring them to life for you and individualize them as interesting and distinctive characters.

Be alert for conflicts that may develop between your characters and explore the reasons for them and how they came about. At this stage you're not writing for publication, so you can feel as free as you like in whatever you set down. Some of it you'll use, some of it you'll discard. The important thing is that the characters will become real in your own mind and be ready to take over when you bring them onstage.

OUTLINE

This is the last of the three major sections of my notebook. Under this heading I ease into the overall framework of the story. Although I have by this time jotted down pages of unconnected ideas, and have written expansively and extensively about my characters, and have some concept of the plot, I don't as yet know a great deal about my scene-by-scene story action.

It's not necessary to know exactly where you're going at the start. The layman often thinks that a "plot" must occur to a writer in a flash, full-blown, but it doesn't usually happen that way. Sometimes I'm not even sure of my villain in the beginning, and may try several characters in that role before I find what will work best for this story.

This *Outline* section helps me to find out where in general the novel is going, without my having to do whole chapters of actual writing. It is here in my notebook that I begin to *organize* all the scattered material I've collected in the other sections under Characters, Situation, Theme, and Plot. Working on the outline is the last step before I actually begin to write, and it is valuable as a guide. I never feel that I am using myself up in this preparatory work; I am only dealing with a plan, a map. The excitement and interest will still be generated when I begin to write. This may not, however, be true for everyone. As always, you must find the way that is comfortable for you.

For the outline, I break down whatever material I have into rough chapters. This can be quite arbitrary and commits me to nothing firm, since I'm only searching for my best overall direction. This bit of action that I've noted under *Plotting* may go here in Chapter I; another might fit into Chapter VIII. This is where the indexing I've mentioned becomes valuable. Something I've elaborated on under *Plotting, P. 10, Item C,* needn't be written out again in this *Outline* section. I simply refer to "10C," placing the identifying number in the proper chapter of the outline.

Next I decide when and where each character is to be introduced. Some of my story people will come onstage in the first chapter. Others must wait until some later, opportune moment. It's not a good idea to throw too many characters at your reader all at once. Careful planning under *Outline* will help you avoid this.

Up to this point, I will not have dealt with the overall plan of my novel, waiting instead until I have enough material for the course of the story to become apparent to me. As I break down whatever I've collected into scenes that will appear in each chapter, I begin to find the shape of my novel and can decide what happens when and where. I am now thinking in *scenes,* and visualization becomes very important. *Plotting* is a collection of ideas. The *Characters* section deals with the people. But in *Outline* the whole thing begins to take shape.

Not everyone will want to do this much planning in a notebook, and when the strong urge to write comes, it's best to give in and start the real task of writing. It's not necessary to know everything before you start. In fact, it's more fun if you can surprise yourself with unexpected turns as you go along. The embroidering of detail always comes as I write, and I never expect a chapter to turn out exactly as I planned it. Yet this first thinking in scene form in my notebook *Outline* is what spurs my imagination to create those details that I will need to bring the story to life.

Whether you plot forward from the beginning, or backward from the end, will depend on what seems best for you. My own imagination will work only with the chronological approach. I may not know all the details of my climax scene until I get there, though my *Outline* gives me its direction and a general idea of what must happen, as well as where it happens.

Unfortunately, there are some editors these days who don't want to read a finished novel until they've seen an outline and can give the author a "go-ahead." I dislike this approach, both because I don't know exactly what's going to happen until I write it, and because I don't think an outline can ever do justice to a book. But since, realistically, this may be a requirement you'll have to meet, you may be able to take care of it in your notebook.

When the urge to write begins to consume me, I go to my typewriter and take the plunge. I no longer have the fear of writing myself out in a few chapters—even if I'm starting too soon—because my notebook is always waiting, and when the desire to write fades (as is quite likely to happen more than once along the way), I simply return to my notebook. I read about my characters again, read through the many pages of my *Plotting* section, to see how more of it will fit into the *Outline*. New ideas come and my plan fleshes out until I can't wait to get back to my typewriter and push ahead again for as long as I can.

While I am outlining in my notebook, I make it a point not to do any of the actual writing. In fact, very little of what I have set down in my notebook so far is used in a novel as it stands. I've been recording ideas, not trying for polished writing. There are only bits and pieces that I can sometimes use as written.

Under the chapter numerals in the *Outline* section, I may set down some such items as I did for *Vermilion*.

I. Scene on deck of guest house in Sedona. Flashback to New York. Lindsay's background. Introduce Rick and mention Sybil's unpleasantness. Touch on Jed's death and bring in Vermilion. Letter that brings L. to Arizona. She decides to go.

II. Arrival in Arizona. Rick changed—remote. Something wrong. Drive to Sedona (background), meeting with Sybil and Brian. Describe house. Close flashback to where Lindsay is on guest house deck, as in opening. Marilla comes to see her unexpectedly.

None of this means anything to anyone but me. It was only intended to indicate possible action. When I wrote (and rewrote) the first chapters, these events were rearranged so that I began in New York and then moved to Arizona. And I got Jed's death into the first sentence.

Time spent on these three main sections of the notebook always makes the actual writing easier, more fluent. My imagination seems to work better when I've given it a great deal to feed on.

There are a few more supplementary headings I include in my notebook:

TO BE CHECKED

If you do any research for your book, factual questions about certain details will come up. Don't count on remembering to look up the answers. Set down the questions as they occur to you and look up the answers when you have time. It's important to be accurate, so question your facts constantly, painstakingly, and be sure to get them right.

BIBLIOGRAPHY

Keep a record of the books you have used, or referred to, in your research. Note the title, author, edition (if applicable). Whether they are from a public library or your own bookshelves, you may need to return to them for further checking. How often I've despaired because I couldn't remember where I'd read something that later became important to know.

RESEARCH

Here I record the notes I make during my reading. For *Vermilion* I made long pages of notes on Indian drums, on the Hopi Indians of Arizona, and even notes on fashion designing. Only a small fraction of this research was used, but because I have it recorded on my loose-leaf pages in the notebook, as I wrote the book I could refer to what I wanted easily. In a subtle way the material in such notes will creep into your writing and add to its richness and texture.

Don't throw any of these notes away when you've finished your novel. For years I've kept extra notebooks in which these loose-leaf *Research* pages are filed under appropriate headings. Years later, in writing another book, I may find such notes useful again, and I'm able to look up the subjects in alphabetical listings.

The collecting of special knowledge with which to enhance and give authenticity to your novels is useful and should go on all the time. Train yourself to notice interesting articles in magazines or newspapers and clip them for your general file. Watch for the unusual book that might prove useful. Years ago I bought an illustrated book on Japanese netsuke . . . an art that has always fascinated me. (Netsuke are miniature ivory carvings used to attach pouches and other objects to the obi, when the men of Japan still wore kimonos.) It took twenty-five years before a character in *Poinciana* turned out to have a netsuke collection, and I could introduce something out of the ordinary into the story.

BACKGROUND

In this section I file any rough plans I draw up for houses, neighborhood, town, area—anything I need to visualize clearly. It's disconcerting when a character goes in one direction to reach a certain place, and then in an opposite direction in another scene—though the goal is the same.

I also write bits of description here that may or may not fit into my story, but which concern the setting.

Since a change of setting provides a change of pace and picks up interest for the reader, I find it useful to list in this section various settings within my main locale that I may use in my story. When I look down such a list, it often sparks my imagination and sets me off on new roads while I'm still in the planning stage. In outlining, it is especially helpful to think of your action as happening in a certain place. You are looking for variety, change, and such a list, thought about ahead of time, will help you.

NAMES

I have kept a permanent place in my notebook for collecting names. Any time I hear an interesting name, I write it down. Last names, first names, foreign names, etc. When I am naming my characters, I often find this list useful.

For me, the greatest value in this notebook system is that it always gives me something to work on, and the notes I am writing in one section keep sparking ideas for another. It's the most painless way of plotting that I've found.

However, if you happen to be the sort of writer who likes to start off adventurously without settling on a direction—that is certainly your privilege, and you'll find your own road eventually. There is never only one way to get there. But if you get lost, if you start to founder, then you might come back and read these notebook chapters again, in case there are ideas here that will help you with problems that develop.

I would like to close with an important warning to those writers who find my notebook system useful. It's fine as far as it goes. But like research, it can become so fascinating to work with that you have the illusion that you're writing a novel, and you let it go on for too long a period. Don't fool yourself. You're not writing a novel until you put *Chapter One* on paper and go on from there into the real writing of your story. A notebook is a valuable tool, but the time must come when you go to your typewriter—and write!

5

THE PLUS FACTOR
That Certain Something

Suppose, for the sake of example, that we take two writers, A and B. Neither one is a "genius," or even a "literary" writer. Both have written long enough to collect a good many rejection slips and also to have learned something about the craft of writing. Both have reached about the same level of achievement in the handling of fiction techniques. Their story characters are reasonably convincing. They write about problems that are important to these characters. There are struggle, conflict, suspense, a good climax and denouement. But somehow there are no sales except for an occasional one to some low-paying or hard-up market.

Then suddenly, A begins to sell regularly to markets he had never been able to reach before, while B goes right on collecting rejection slips. Naturally, B develops a grudge against the injustice of editors. He knows he is as skilled a craftsman, can write as readable a story, is in fact every bit as good a writer as A. Why can't he sell his stuff more regularly?

The answer lies in three words: "as good as . . ." "As good as" always spells mediocrity. But when a writer's work is in competition with all those thousands of other manuscripts that pour over an editor's desk, he cannot afford to be "as good as"; he (or she) must be "better than."

When you explain this to B, he makes impolite noises. Sure, sure, he'd just love to be better than the next writer, but right now he's doing the best he can. He knows it's not a bad job, and if he could rate a pull with an editor the way A does—well, he'd start selling all his stuff, too. But you know how it is, editors play favorites, and what chance does a writer stand when he lives way out in Deep Prairie where he never even sees or gets to talk to an editor? (Or maybe he lives in New York City, where writers are a dime a dozen, and few editors have time to talk to you anyway if you're a beginner.)

To a certain extent, editors do play favorites. And A may manage to rate a "pull." Editors have an admitted weakness for the writer who turns out the story, the book, that has a plus factor, and they'll play favorites with that writer everytime. But the plus factor is just as available to B as it is to A; all he has to do is invest a bit more time and thought in his stories in the preparatory stage, recognizing exactly what a plus factor is, so that he can inject it into his own writing.

For several years, I spent a day every two weeks reading manuscripts for one of my own publishers in New York. Since they specialized in the juvenile field, I read book manuscripts written for young people, and

I discovered then how the plus factor shines out in any story. This is no different in adult writing.

There are a large number of stories that are just plain bad. A publisher's reader disposes of those in a hurry. There are a smaller number in that pitiful "as good as" group—stories that might be saved, if only the writer would wake up. And then there are the wonderful few in which the plus factor makes itself evident very quickly, and the first reader settles down for a pleasant time with something he can pass along to his editor.

Editors are interested in the plus factor because they are in competition with other publishers. All publishing houses want books that will bring fan mail from readers, that will make reviewers sit up and take notice. They are looking for stories that readers will tell one another about, novels they will flock into stores to buy, and to libraries to borrow. No editor can afford to publish the book or story that is only "as good as," any more than a writer can afford to produce it.

So, way back in the beginning, when B is thinking about the story he is going to write, he must ask himself how he can make his story or book stand out and really hook the reader's interest. How can he make his story *different?* "Different" is perhaps a misleading word because the novice may take it to mean bizarre, and the bizarre is seldom wanted. A story of ordinary people set in an average American town can be "different," can have the plus factor that recommends it to the reader.

I spent almost four years collecting rejection slips before I discovered the magic wand that was right there all the time, waiting for me to pick it up. The moment I reached for it, I began to sell. At the time, I was trying for two separate markets: the church paper field and the "love pulps." I had lived in the Orient until I was fifteen, and I remembered my life there very well. But since that was my own backyard, I didn't want to write about it. Someone with better sense urged me to try, and I found that the Sunday School papers were eager for stories about American young people in Japan and the Philippines and China. I had found a plus factor, and my stories began to sell as fast as I could write them.

But the Orient is certainly not the answer for everyone. The thing our friend B needs to discover is that Deep Prairie will give him that plus factor too. And so will Cleveland or New York City, Evanston, Illinois, or San Antonio, Texas. It will give it to him in two different ways. First, because he knows more about his own backyard than the other fellow does. Second, because the other fellow always thinks somebody else's backyard is more interesting than his own, and a large reader segment is hooked. On the other hand, those who live, or *have ever been* in Deep Prairie, love to read about scenes they have visited, and they offer a basic reading audience.

Discovering the value of my own background may have helped as far as the educational papers went, but the love story magazines felt their readers didn't want to read about faraway places. It's very different now, when exotic backgrounds are popular, but then it was thought that American readers wanted to read only about America. In casting about for another plus factor, I hit on the idea of writing "job stories." That is, I would pick some line of work that my heroine might be in. Then I'd do some research on this job or profession, and use that as the plus factor for my story. I wrote about a girl who owned a perfume shop, about a lovelorn columnist, a newspaper reporter, and so on endlessly. Each story had freshness and flavor because I became so involved and interested in the subject I was investigating that I *made it my own* before I wrote the story.

When I began writing books for teen-agers, it was simple enough to go right on with this same basic idea by fitting myself into the "career" book field that was very big at that time. My second book, *A Star for Ginny,* was about a girl who sold books in a department store. *A Window for Julie* was about window decorating in a big store. I found the latter background so fascinating that I wrote an adult mystery novel, *Red Is for Murder,* using the same background. This sold so few copies that I gave up on the adult field for a good many years—only to have the book revived later in paper, where it still sells very well as *The Red Carnelian.*

There were countless variations possible with this "job" type of plus factor, and I found it always interesting to utilize—and still do, to some extent. However, I didn't want to use that one story "trick" alone all the rest of my writing life, so after I had finished my fifth career book, I cast around for a new plus factor. And that was when I happened on the most important "secret" of all.

As a reviewer of children's books, I'd read the best of what was being published, and now I set out to discover what constituted a "better book." I found out: It was nearly always a book that said something worth saying. *Said something.* That was what made certain books stand out over so many others! Significance, meaning, a message, not the obvious, not just the same clichés.

Off I went in search of something to say. I found my first theme in the prejudice that existed when Negroes (we didn't say "blacks" in those days) moved into a new neighborhood and found themselves unwanted. I dug in for long and solid research on the subject, and along the way the thing happened that *must* happen if you are to succeed. I was already sympathetic toward this subject, but now I forgot all about the fact that this might be a way of earning money, or getting my books better known. I found myself emotionally involved in the problem I was studying. I'd have written that book whether it sold or not. In fact, my editor told me she was not interested in the subject, and felt that it wouldn't "sell." (How wrong she was!) I decided to write it anyway and take it elsewhere. On the first writing, I was so lost in my theme that I was up on a soapbox preaching, instead of telling a story. I had to do it all over, so that my characters and what happened to them would carry my "message." The book was *Willow Hill*, which won a prize and is still in print because, unfortunately, some of the same problems it dealt with continue to exist.

If you don't have this emotional involvement, throw the subject away. You can't fake conviction. Whatever you want to say in your fiction must come out of what you believe and feel. Examine your own beliefs first of all. You might write down a list of subjects that you feel strongly about and add to it constantly, since this will make an excellent source for story ideas you may want to develop.

I began to write other "problem" novels. Not always social problems, but stories that dealt with the difficult

personal problems faced by young people. Human
problems. The fan mail I still get shows how eagerly
such stories are received. Here is a quote from a girl's
letter that I still treasure:

> One of the reasons I like your books is that the
> people in your books have the same problems
> that other people do, and then they find a way
> out of them.

This reaction comes in different words from adult
readers, too.

These days in my writing I try to offer, as a "plus
factor," something unusual in the way of background
or profession, and something significant in what my
characters must learn in the course of the story—always remembering that reading fiction should be entertaining, and that I must first tell a good story.

In *The Golden Unicorn,* my heroine had been
adopted, and she sets out to discover her real parents.
This required knowledge that I didn't have in the
beginning. I needed to learn about the laws that gov-
ern adoption, and even more important, I had to understand the psychological impact upon those who are
adopted. Also to be considered were the feelings of
the mother who gave her child away. Thus what is
essentially a mystery-suspense novel also has something to say about a perennial human problem.

Sometimes a subject you have already explored and
put a good deal of time into can be used again in a
different way. Five books later, in *Vermilion,* I've written about a young woman who is fearful of learning
who her mother is, so that she resists this information
until it is forced upon her. Different human beings

react differently and can give you totally different stories.

Your plus factor can be anything that will add dimension, a "certain something" to your writing. It's that "certain something" that every editor is looking for.

6

USING "THE FORCE"

The movie *Star Wars* entranced me with its magical aspects and gave me a name for something I've been using all my writing life: *The Force.* I could easily believe that such a power emanated from Alec Guinness as Obi-Wankenobi as I watched him on the screen.

In my case, however, it is an inner resource that I tap to stimulate my creativeness, and not a power to direct at others.

There is growing interest these days in the functions of the left and right sides of the brain. What interests me most in this is not the scientific discussion, but the means by which I can get the creative side of my brain to function in my own work.

I used to call this faculty "inspiration," and I used it instinctively, almost unconsciously. I didn't know how to coax it into working on demand when I most needed it. As a result, there were sometimes long dry periods during which the imaginative flow ceased. I wasn't suffering from true "writer's block"; I could write, and I did, but with no great satisfaction or confidence in what I was doing. The process was too mechanical.

Gradually, as I read about ways creative people have used this resource, I began to put into practice the methods by which I, too, could utilize its power. I learned to make it a constant element in my writing. If you haven't explored this, you can start right away collecting the means of stimulating this creative flow. As you read and listen, and learn how other creative people work (not only writers), you can adapt their methods to your own use.

Of course there are many writers whose creativity is active all the time, and they have only to put their fingers on the typewriter keys for words to pour out. Such writers are, as a rule, enormously prolific, and they can often write with very little advance planning. I'm not like that, and I had to find a more conscious method by which to stimulate the unconscious, creative stream.

Though I've always felt that I *had* to write, there were many times in my early days when I didn't like writing; I liked only "to have written." Today—most of the time—I can count on a gratifying flow of ideas (stimulated by the work in my notebook). When the flow fails me, it may be that I'm not listening to my own inner voices. When there's a balking, it usually means that I'm going down a wrong road, and had better stop to re-examine, to search out what is wrong, and develop a new approach. I've learned not to ignore that warning voice that makes me feel uneasy.

In order to put this "Force" to its fullest use, there are three practical steps to be taken. You'll find these same steps mentioned again and again in writings on creativity.

1. Put raw material into your mind. Ask questions.

2. Give yourself time for this to be "processed."

3. Examine what has come into your mind to find the answers.

This sounds simple enough, and to a degree it is; it really works, and there's nothing mystical about it. How well it works is probably a matter of training, of conditioning. There are special approaches involved in each of the three steps.

Putting the raw material into your mind is fascinating and rewarding. The more you feed in, the more likely it is that the "unconscious" factor will take over when you need it. New ideas will then flow generously into your conscious mind and enrich your writing. A mind empty of new information will take you nowhere, so there must always be this fresh input.

Once you've fed information into your mind, you can ask yourself the *specific questions* that your conscious mind can't answer. These may take any form, be any of the unanswered problems concerning plot, character—anything at all that you need to solve before you write.

One useful means I've found that gives me the right questions to ask, is very simple. I keep a running list of questions during the time when I'm working on my notebook. When I begin, there are a lot of elementary questions to ask myself. Later these become more complex. It helps me to write them down and then read through the list every day to see which questions have been answered and can be crossed out, and which I need to feed into my mind with special emphasis today. Just setting down the questions is a productive step toward finding the answers I need.

Once you've put information and one or two questions into your mind, take the second step. Go for a walk, go to sleep, do other things, until some time has passed. There's no telling how long it will take. Sometimes I have an answer to my questions in five minutes; other times it can take weeks. It has seemed to me that the *urgency* of my need, the desperation with which I regard a certain problem, can really speed up the response. But if it won't come, turn to other sections of your notebook, where there is always work to be done.

Buried somewhere in your unshaped collection of ideas, or even in the chapters you've already written, will lie the clues that your unconscious will recognize and pounce upon. Often when the flash of ideas comes to me well on in the writing, I find that I must go back and write in new material to support the change. Oddly enough, this is easy to do because the source of the illuminating flash nearly always grows from something already planted much earlier in my novel. I hadn't recognized it with my conscious mind until now. Once I do, it's easy to find the right place for it in the story, and the difficult obstacle surmounted, I'm on my way again.

Often you can get this process started by reversing something in your characters or plot. Choose a new direction, provoke your story people, set them against one another. Ask yourself "what if . . ." and then leave them to stew. You must always allow for that "stewing" period before you can expect answers.

But this doesn't mean that you can't make the third step and take it out to examine whenever you please. If no answers come, put it back and forget about it again. The third step is as important as the others—re-examining. You must look at the questions deliberately from time to time. Sooner or later the answers come, and you can perhaps go in some marvelous new direction that your conscious mind had never expected you to take, but which you'll deal with eagerly, once the answer is revealed.

It is there in you, that Force that can help you create, help you solve your most difficult writing problems. Discover how to use it—and practice!

PART TWO
TECHNIQUE

7

BEGINNINGS, MIDDLES, AND ENDINGS

Until now, I've been discussing approaches to writing—the preliminaries. We've been talking about preparation, about getting ready to write. Real life, however, doesn't divide itself as neatly as a book on writing. You've probably been working all along, and doing it in your own way—which must always feel right for you. My purpose is to help you shorten the time between when you are a "beginning" writer and when you become a "professional," selling writer.

The chapters in this second section will deal with writing techniques. These are the skills I have been studying for a long time, and which I use constantly in my own work. If I had known more about such skills when I started out, my period of hit-or-miss struggles needn't have gone on for so long. Though even when you know, it takes practice to do it all well.

If you are already working on a notebook, as I've suggested, this is the time when you stop all preparation, leave the fun and security of your notebook behind. There is the danger that working on a notebook can come to mean safety. It gives us the illusion that we're really working, yet we can actually be postponing that frightening day when we must risk all by getting down to the actual writing of the novel. I never start a new book without feeling intimidated by those boxes of empty typing paper. How can I possibly ever write that many words again?

It's easy. We need only to write one page at a time. For all the months of writing that lie ahead, that's all that's required of us—one page, and then another. It's astonishing how they pile up.

Besides, you aren't putting your notebook away, or closing it forever. It is still there to be used as the map you've devised for your journey. While there is very little in my notebook that I lift out to use "as is" in the actual writing, I incorporate its *ideas* constantly. It is always there to guide me, to keep me from forgetting, and to help my imagination stay afire.

BEGINNINGS

Probably the best way to start any story, long or short, is to show *a character with a problem doing something interesting.* The more quickly you can make what is happening clear, the more likely you'll be to draw your reader into your story.

The old questions that have always been set down in books on writing are still necessary to consider: *Who? What? Where? When? Why?* It's seldom easy to answer all of them quickly and gracefully in those first pages. Expect to do your beginning over several times. Often, when I have the rest of my novel finished, I am still rewriting the opening. It won't go away—you can come back to it at any time if it doesn't suit you now.

You will need to involve the reader quickly with your viewpoint character, arouse curiosity, and give the casual browser who picks up your book a feeling that he or she *must* know more about what this character is doing and why. Long expositions, descriptions, philosophizing, may entertain you, but are unlikely to grip a busy reader today. In the past we could be more leisurely.

When I start writing a first chapter, I am disturbingly aware of the quantity of information that must be presented before my readers can begin to understand what I'm talking about. I usually write a first opening in which I explain everything and get it off my chest. Only then can I read it through and decide which parts of this mass of explanation are really needed *right now*. I always find that much of it can be postponed. The reader doesn't have to know everything right away. Yet he mustn't be left in a state of confusion either. So identify the *Who*, the *Where*, the *When*, and even the *What* as quickly and briefly as possible. It's the *Why* that is going to give you trouble, and you don't have to cope with all of that right away.

Let's examine a few of my opening paragraphs. From *Poinciana:*

> Outside the long windows of the library, a Florida March was mild, almost balmy. Sunset light touched the fine book bindings, turning polished mahogany rosy, but I sat well away from the win-

dows, huddled in a wing chair and hidden by the deepest shadow I could find.

The *Where:* an apparently luxurious library in a private home in Florida; the *When:* a balmy March, sunset; a possible *Who;* and *What* she is doing. The *Why* is hinted at by a question the reader will ask—why is she huddling in shadow? We hope the reader may want to find out more.

From *Vermilion:*

> The first step that would take me to Arizona began at the time of Jed Phillips's murder.

This doesn't tell very much, but it presents some of the *Why* at once. It flings down a challenge and makes the reader go on to the next paragraph, which tells a lot more.

From *The Glass Flame:*

> I was only a few miles from Gatlinburg when the sign pointing right caught my eye: *Belle Isle.* I hadn't intended to stop until I reached Trevor Andrew's house, but the name compelled me. This was the place to which my husband, David Hallam, had come. This was where he had died. His burying still lay ahead of me with all the problems and questions it would involve.

In my own books those present in the first scene *(Who),* plus the "I" of first person, can be mentioned quickly. Then as we move on in the story, we come to meet the characters in greater detail.

In the above paragraph from *The Glass Flame,* we

have a specific place *(Where)*, but not yet the time of year or day *(When)*, though that will come shortly (as it should). The *What* is clear. She's driving a car. The *Why* is suggested strongly, and we sense trouble to come. (Always a good idea in any opening.) Bit by bit I will now make the *Who* clear.

From *Secret of the Missing Footprint* (a juvenile mystery):

> The day I met Timothy Rainbow my whole life changed. I don't suppose I'll ever be the same again. At first, even though he fascinated me, I thought he was a dangerous boy. In the end . . .
> But I can't tell you sensibly about the end until you understand the beginning.

This is almost all about *Who*, and perhaps the reader will go along with a little necessary explanation that follows.

In every one of these openings a serious problem has been hinted at. You will clarify as you continue but you do need to suggest a problem immediately, whatever sort of novel you mean to write. The *Why* of your opening always involves a problem.

If you can present an arresting beginning, then you can slow down the pace a little for some of the explanation that must be fitted into the following paragraphs. Get into action—something *happening*—as soon as possible, and weave in information along the way, avoiding solid clumps that do not dramatize what is happening.

When you try for an arresting opening, however, beware of overdramatic action. Readers aren't interested in watching people they don't know run around frantically doing something that isn't clear. If you've ever tuned into the middle of a fight or a car chase on television, you know how boring fast action can be when the emotions are not first involved. *Involvement* is the key word.

While you were working in your notebook, you met your characters at a superficial level, gradually deepening them as you got to know them better. But you were merely talking to yourself about them. Now you bring them onstage where you can watch them act, listen to them talk, learn what they are thinking. You'll want to make them interesting quickly in your opening scenes, so that the reader will want to know more about them and continue reading. Writing a novel is really *finding your story, finding your people, discovering what you want to say.* The notebook is a springboard, but it's never the final novel.

In your opening, you will need to establish the immediate problem that faces your main character. You will also make it clear why your character can't solve this problem easily. The reader must know what obstacles lie in the pathway to solution (though not all of them at once—let these develop through the story); how difficult they are to solve, and what conflicts are likely to arise that will keep your heroine or hero from the goal of the climax scene. This sequence is likely to be repeated all the way through your book as there are defeats and successes, and new problems arise.

A "plot" is the facing and solving of a difficult main problem, so don't let the word frighten you.

How long the beginning of your novel goes on, and where the middle starts, is an arguable point. Perhaps it doesn't matter, and you will move automatically from beginning, to middle, without needing to know any exact demarcation. Nor is there any set length for beginnings. Some are long, some very short. However, lest you wander on and on, without really getting your story started, there is a test you can make, which will tell you whether you are coming to grips with what must be done.

Much of the beginning will be concerned with establishing who the characters are; what has happened earlier, before the story starts, to lead to this predicament; what is happening now; what the main problem of the story is likely to be; and who and what opposes your main character. When you tell the reader that the main character has decided to *act*, to do something about the problem, then your beginning ends, and you move into the middle of your book. A story beginning, in which the main character is merely trying to decide what to do, can become tiresome if it goes on too long. So keep in mind that the first move the character makes to work out what confronts him should come fairly early in the novel, so that you leave the beginning behind and get into the important action.

MIDDLES

Middles are hard. The first bloom of your love affair with this story is over. Most of the pages of your novel lie in the middle, and must be struggled through somehow. The ending is far ahead, and you are quickly losing touch with what lies behind. Inevitably, there's a lessening of your self-confidence as enthusiasm wanes. The weakening self-questioning starts. Should you really be writing this novel? Maybe it isn't any good, after all, and you ought to start something else? (Never listen to this one!) Perhaps you shouldn't even try to finish this horrible mess? (More of the same!) When these feelings become so strong that they are holding you back, stop and take time to read through everything you've written to this point.

It's never a good idea to reread the whole thing through constantly, though you may be tempted to do so. Stay away from that. I like to have fifty to a hundred pages behind me before I stop for this first complete rereading. While you're writing, you should be satisfied to reread *only* whatever you wrote the day before. You do this in order to recapture your mood, reacquaint yourself with what happened last, and thus regain impetus to move ahead with the next scene. It's safer not to read back any more than that, however great the temptation, until you have some real wordage behind you. You need to have the rereading come to you fresh when you've been away from it for a while.

When you do come to this first real rereading, you will probably find that it's not as bad as you feared. Your confidence and eagerness to move ahead will return, and you'll be on your way again.

It is at this point, when you're ready to write again, that you can return to your notebook and find help for the chapters that still lie ahead. With some of the story written, you are in a better position to plan a few more chapters—always sketchily, so you don't write yourself out in the outline. As you reread the pages of the Development section, you can now see that this will fit here, and that somewhere else, while another item may be discarded altogether. New ideas keep coming, and you enter them, so that the form of your novel fleshes out still more as you move ahead.

It's a good idea at this point to go through all your

character sketches again. You may feel that you know your story people well enough by now, but you're still likely to find points in those sketches that have slipped your mind, and that you can now use to good effect.

Your eagerness to write will return in full force, as it always does when the larder is well-stocked, and you'll be ready to write again. In another hundred pages, you may find that you'll need to stop and repeat this refresher process. It will always revive your interest and spur you on.

A word about story scenes might be appropriate here, since most of your scenes will take place in the middle of a novel.

For me, a scene is a unit of action that takes place with one grouping of characters in one setting. Of course other actors may join your scene, or even leave it, but the setting stays the same, giving it coherence: a room, a garden, a house that characters are moving through, a beach, a mountain path—whatever you choose for a setting. Even a moving car or plane is in itself a scene setting, though the landscape outside may change.

No scene should remain static, without movement or action, however small it may sometimes be if people are sitting in a room conversing. There should be movement of plot, even if not of people, and a furthering of, or setback to, the character's present problem. I will touch on this in greater detail later.

The best way for me to handle a scene, is to visualize it as if it were taking place on a stage. Then I can watch everything the characters do, and listen to what they say as well. Unlike a play, however, I can also get inside my main character's thoughts, or the thoughts of other characters if I am using more than one viewpoint.

During the writing of this long middle of your book, you will find (should find) that there is an almost automatic building to small climaxes along the way. The course of your story is somewhat up and down, with a problem solved or defeated, and new problems arising, though with an overall steadily mounting climb that will lead you at last to the climax of your novel.

CLIMAX AND ENDING-CONCLUSION

These are two separate phases of your conclusion. One may be fairly long, the other should be as short as possible.

The climax scene is the high point of your story. It is the scene in which everything comes to a final test—a showdown—and the last effort is made by the main character, or characters, to meet the enemy in victory or defeat. *It should certainly be played out dramatically onstage.* This is an important warning. You can't afford to skip your climax scene, or your readers will not feel satisfied. Again and again, manuscripts have come to me in which the writer, coming face to face with the test of writing the Big Scene (and doubting his ability to handle it), skips ahead to a scene later in time, and has someone describe in retrospect what has happened. This is fatal. The climax scene is the most important confrontation in your book, and you will need to give it your best dramatic *onstage* presentation. It is the reward your reader has been waiting for, so don't cheat him of this satisfaction.

During the climax scene a number of balls must be kept in the air up to the very last moment. Then catch them all neatly, and quickly write *The End*. If one of them (some unexplained point) rolls under the sofa, never to be seen again, your reader will be annoyed. This is the place where all those loose ends must be neatly tied up in a way that is convincing and will still not slow the action. Keeping curiosity high by dangling a carrot in front of the reader is the way to do it, though this can be tricky to manage. Count on writing the last scene, and probably the ending, over several times.

The hardest part of a mystery novel for most suspense writers is to account for all those red herrings and loose ends. Keep a list of them along the way, as they're easy to overlook in the long time it takes to write a novel. Explain as much as possible *before* the actual climax scene. This is easier to do when you're writing in the third person and can break to other viewpoints—characters who may know more about what's been happening than your main character does. In my books, since I write in first person these days, and have always written from a single viewpoint, this becomes difficult to do. I dislike having the villain stand still and explain everything at the end, and I constantly try to play variations on this theme. Yet I've never completely resolved this difficulty to my own satisfaction. All I can do is try to cut down on the explanations, get as much as possible in ahead of time, keeping the climax scene dramatic and suspenseful, while explanations are being woven in. If you're not writing a mystery, climax explanations are much easier to handle.

When you deal with a theme in the course of your novel—that is, something you want your main character to learn or prove by the end of your book—it is in the climax or final scene that everything must be made clear. Subtly, please. You must *show* through action and characters that there has been learning and growth, or deterioration—whatever it is you set out to reveal.

Whether your ending is happy or unhappy depends on you. Since I am writing to entertain, to bring a lift of spirit at the end of my novels, they always have "happy" endings. You have every right to see what you are doing in a different light, and you may feel that the only "realistic" ending is a tragic one for your story. Tragedy can have a larger purpose when it illuminates the human experience.

Often the young are more given to tragic endings than are older writers. Teen-agers, in particular, can be startlingly gruesome. Perhaps those of us who have suffered enough real-life disasters, feel that we want to offer hope at the end of our stories. We may even feel that hope can be rewarding—something the teen-ager may not believe in his own frequently unhappy state of life. For me, a lifting of the spirits at the end of a work of fiction is an especially satisfying experience. I don't want to deny it to my readers.

The real test may lie in the word "satisfaction." As a reader, when I am convinced that a character *deserves* what happens at the end, an emotional satisfaction results, and the ending seems right. If the main characters have struggled through all their vicissitudes and come out on top, then I feel satisfied that they deserved to win.

On the other hand, if I can see all through a story that the main character is digging persistently the pit of his own destruction, then he, too, may deserve what he gets at the end, and there is still reader satisfaction, as well as that illumination of the human experience.

Recently I read in galleys an excellent suspense novel by a very good writer. Her characters (the two main characters) had courage and intelligence, and were attractive people. They met their terrible predicament with effort and ingenuity. There was goodness and nobility here, standing against forces of evil. By the end of the story I was cheering for them to win. The climax scene carried high suspense, and these two people were very near to freedom and safety. But the author shot them both dead in the final scene—and I threw the book across the room! This, I claim, is not the way to satisfy a reader. This man and woman didn't deserve what happened to them, and as a reader I did not want them to die.

You have to decide what sort of novel you want to write. Perhaps more than anything else, it is the discovery of self that counts most, whether for our characters or for ourselves. If no editor wants your manuscript, or if, when it is published, no one likes it, and you are feeling discouraged and unhappy, perhaps you have only yourself to blame, and you've failed in providing reader-satisfaction.

On one thing I hope you will be sure to take my advice. When you come to the end, when the story is over—stop! All too often in beginners' manuscripts, superfluous actions are tacked on after the story is over.

As I said earlier, *Climax* and *Ending* are two different things. The Climax is the big dramatic scene in which almost everything is resolved. The Ending is the wrap-up where lovers used to embrace and walk happily into the sunset. If possible, it's a good idea to leave a thread of question in the reader's mind right up to the last paragraph. Then let the sun go down fast, give your blessings to your characters and let them go. Let your whole book go. After all, another novel is waiting to be written, and you are eager to get to it!

8

SUSPENSE

To paraphrase Stephen King in his splendid book on horror writing, *Danse Macabre*, a novel without a plot is like a car without an engine—it won't run. Too often, as King points out, the so-called "literary" story may lack the machine parts to get it on the road. Suspense is an important element in the machinery, and the good mystery and suspense writer can be studied with profit, whether you want to write that specific type of novel or not. Suspense is vital to every kind of fiction writing.

Tension is the element that keeps the reader turning the pages, and to have tension, you must build suspense. Both grow from many variables that are discussed in other chapters of this book, but four ingredients are of paramount importance: Problem, Purpose, Conflict, Goal.

All four are necessary. Three are fairly obvious, and anyone who means to write fiction is aware of the fact that there must be a *problem,* there must be *conflict* (or difficulties), and there must be a *goal* that the character wants to reach. *Purpose* is hardly ever discussed, yet it is one of the prime essentials if you want to keep interest high *in every scene.*

A working definition of "purpose" as I use it here is *an attempt to resolve.* A problem and a goal may exist, but until the main character has an active purpose, and takes action to resolve some problem, there will be little reader interest. Even in a short story there are problems within an individual scene that lead eventually to the solution of the main problem. Your main character must take some action toward resolving these problems. There must be a purpose to drive your hero or heroine into action.

Every piece of fiction should start with a state of crisis, out of which future action grows. This crisis must affect and be resolved by the action of the main character; it can't be someone else's problem or solution. From the point at the outset when the crisis situation is presented, every scene must have problem, purpose and goal. There must always be difficulties in your hero's path, and these usually, but not always, contain conflict—including conflicts that can occur within the character.

The developing of an *active* purpose for your main character is not easy. Unless I am careful, I frequently find that all sorts of problems—both my heroine's and those of other characters—are latent but not apparent. Or else some other character is working at *his* problem, while the heroine watches passively, as if she had no problem of her own—in which case she drifts along, just letting things happen *to* her. When this is the situation, there is no purpose, no "attempt to resolve" on the part of the main character, and reader interest is likely to lag.

Purpose is something you must consider deliberately to make sure it exists in every scene. It always leads to action and makes the reader want to know what will happen next. Of course there should be uncertainty about *what* will happen. The more unexpected, unforeseen, and unpredictable the outcome, the stronger the story interest, the stronger the suspense.

At the beginning of one of my own suspense novels, *Listen for the Whisperer,* the heroine's father had recently died and left a letter for her (Leigh) stating his last wishes: He wants her to go to Norway to find her mother, an actress who abandoned her in infancy and of whom she has no recollection.

Leigh's immediate problem is to decide whether or not to carry out her father's wishes (which are not *her* wishes) and go to Norway to find her mother. If she just thinks about this, the story will be dull. To help her resolve this problem, she *takes action* by going to a theater which is showing an old film starring her movie actress mother, Laura Worth. Leigh's attempt to resolve this indecision is her *purpose.* The motion picture so disturbs her that she rushes from the theater before it ends. The next scene takes place in her father's study at home, and the action she takes is to go through old clippings and look at a picture of her mother, at her father's books, etc. She is thinking, but she is also *doing* something. The conflict is within Leigh herself. She wants to go, and she doesn't want to go. At the end of the scene and the chapter, her initial purpose is satisfied, the immediate problem is settled: She will go to Norway. We know now that her goal is to meet her mother. Curiosity as to what will happen carries the reader into the next chapter. Of such small things may suspense be constructed.

This is not always the case. A piece of fiction may open with a dramatic scene in which problem, purpose, conflict, and goal are immediately apparent and are worked out in exciting action. This way, however, may not always suit the material in hand. A story that is difficult to get into can be helped by having the main character *think* in terms of purpose, of taking some sort of action, however quiet. The main character makes things happen through his or her own action, and there are chain reactions to whatever she does.

There are three ways you may handle purpose and problem.

    1.   Purpose is fulfilled; the problem is solved.

    2.   Purpose is defeated; the problem is not solved.

    3.   The problem is carried over to the next scene, having been neither resolved nor defeated, and a new purpose evolves to deal with the problem.

To accomplish the first, the writer must *immediately* find a new problem about which the main character means to *do* something; that is, your hero or heroine must develop a new purpose. Otherwise, interest drops with the solving of the initial problem. In the second case, the main character is blocked and interest continues as the reader wonders what approach to solving the problem the hero or heroine will use next. If the third occurs, the tension mounts as unexpected complications increase, and the main character continues to work on the problem, attempting to resolve it by new means.

When Leigh reaches Bergen, Norway, her new problem is how to meet her mother. If she does nothing about it, she has no purpose. In the novel, her first purpose in Norway—her immediate action—is to phone her mother's house. She is not allowed to speak to the actress, so we have a defeat of Leigh's purpose, and the problem is not solved. It remains the same, but her purpose in trying to solve it must take a new course. Later in the day, the man her mother is now married to comes to Leigh's hotel to talk to her. Her purpose in the exchange is to persuade him to let her see her mother. He forbids this. Defeat. But Leigh is still trying. Main characters do not give up, and her purpose again takes a new course.

She now seeks out a friend of her father's, a man whom she has been instructed to see if she needs help. He agrees to meet her. The problem changes form, and a new purpose develops for Leigh. Can she persuade this man to help her? He agrees, and they make a plan. Her immediate purpose is fulfilled, and the next attack upon the original (unsolved) problem of meeting her mother must be made. Nothing is standing still. One thing grows from another, and there is no doubt that the heroine has a purpose in each scene. Of course, when she finally meets her mother, still more serious problems arise.

It is not always necessary for the reader to know at once what that purpose is. Occasionally, for the sake of suspense, the writer may postpone making the main character's intention clear to the reader. He may write, "I knew exactly what I must do, and I hurried downstairs to find him." It is enough that the main character knows what *she* is doing, and the reader follows along to find out what her purpose is. The same thing is sometimes true in the opening of a story. The main character is actively engaged in following some intent, but readers don't know immediately what that is. Curiosity carries them along until they find out.

Purpose also lends immediacy. The reader doesn't know what the main problem of the novel will be, but the action is leading toward an answer, and provides something that must be done *right now*. A problem that can be postponed does not produce suspense. Urgency—if possible, a time limit—increases suspense.

Any problem implies a goal that the main character is seeking to reach. The main goal of the story must be desperately important to the character's happiness. Sometimes life or death may depend upon its successful achievement. But not all story goals, problems, and purposes can be equally important. A minor purpose may serve for a single scene, and then the writer goes on to other happenings. We hold our readers' interest while the heroine tries to get her mother on the telephone; we use almost any similar small purpose that will provide action and lead to more momentous events. If you find that the purpose or immediate goal of your main character is weak, limit it to a single scene. Making a phone call isn't all that strong, and it will grow tiresome if Leigh keeps on trying to telephone.

Purpose—that attempt to resolve—is something that can work for you constantly in many ways. It is a good idea to know what the purposes of your other characters are in every scene (whether you tell the reader or not) so that *you* understand exactly what your main character is up against. Your opposition, your "villain," also has a problem, a purpose, a goal, and these will supply additional conflict. As a writer, you must be aware of these elements, set them in your main character's path, and so threaten disaster. Without purpose and cross-purpose, it is too easy for your story to drift, rudderless—and lose the reader.

Purpose that leads directly to achievement (or defeat) is the obvious kind. But there are scenes in which you may find it difficut to have the main character take outward action. Which leads us to the purpose of merely resisting someone or something. When my heroine digs in her heels and refuses to accept what another character wants to achieve through her, or wants to convince her of, that is still an attempt to resolve something: it has purpose.

Leigh is antagonistic toward her mother. She has no sympathy or feeling for her (or so she thinks). Her father's friend likes Laura Worth very much. Leigh doesn't want to be caught by what she regards as his sentimentality, and she attempts to resolve this problem by resisting his sympathy for Laura. She can do nothing except resist it, but resistance means an inner conflict, and this lends interest to the scene.

As every beginning writer is told, there are three kinds of conflict in fiction: Man against man; man against himself; man against nature. I may use all three in a novel. I certainly use the first two. In *Listen for the Whisperer,* Leigh finds herself in conflict with her mother, with the man Laura has married, with other characters in Laura's house, and with her father's friend. She also finds herself very much in conflict with her own ambivalent feelings about her mother. These conflicts lead to new problems, new purposes—and to the eventual goal of reconciliation between the two women, as well as the end of a physical threat to both. There is also a romantic resolution.

Make sure that your main character's purpose is opposed in nearly every scene. This opposition, or conflict, may be intense, or it may be the quiet kind. Variety is needed. How much does your main character want to solve his problem, against what opposition, to reach his goal? What will it cost him if he doesn't succeed? This cost may not be so very great in the beginning, but as the story develops, the main character must find himself trapped (by circumstances, by other people, by his own emotions), so that he can't run away but must stand and fight. Out of these strong emotional situations conflict grows. A problem you can easily ignore doesn't lead to strong story purposes or a life-or-death goal. Unless you give your character the courage to fight, the conflict will do you no good.

How strong is the opposition that makes a solution far from easy? Conflict is especially dramatic when opposite traits clash. Because Leigh finds herself a very different person from her mother, the seeds of conflict are there to be cultivated in many scenes. There are decisions to be made, and the wrong ones will cost Leigh everything she wants. She is surrounded, cornered. She has to act. As tension mounts, other characters force purpose upon her.

As you go from one problem to the next in writing your novel, you must always have in mind an immediate purpose for your main character. The threat of failure that will destroy the main character's happiness, perhaps even her life, should increase, and there should be strong opposition on all sides to raise this threat. Such threats must always be real. *If your oppo-*

sition is only a misunderstanding that could be cleared up at any point, it isn't strong enough. No danger must ever be faked. I see this flaw constantly, even in published novels, and it always weakens the story's suspense. Be sure to test your plot structure for any false threat. (Writers are very good at fooling themselves most of all, as I know well.)

When you raise opposition and conflict, defeat your main character's purposes, and block the solving of problems, it can become monotonous and depressing if it goes on too long. I have read books so filled with continuous disasters that the story was no longer enjoyable. High tension that never lets down can become as monotonous as no tension at all. There must always be the relief of an interlacing of hope. Sometimes, after a struggle, the main character's purpose may seem to succeed completely so there is hope for reaching the ultimate goal of happiness. Of course there's more trouble to come. The "final" answer to the struggle, the solution to the puzzle, mustn't be reached until the end of the novel. Some temporary relief along the way offers a relaxation of tension, though even in quiet scenes your main character should still have a problem, a purpose, a goal.

Is there any time in a piece of fiction when the main character may lack a purpose and have no *immediate* goal? Yes, that can happen, but a fiction writer must be wary of such situations. There is a scene toward the end of *Listen for the Whisperer* in which Leigh, Laura, and several other characters go to see a play at the National Theater in Bergen. This is not Leigh's scene, even though it is described through Leigh's viewpoint. The scene belongs to Laura, who, though once a famous movie star, has not emerged in public for twenty years and is now sitting dramatically in a theater box for all the audience to see.

Leigh is filled with anxiety about her mother and about what has been happening in Laura's house. All sorts of problems remain, but she does not try to change anything herself in this scene. The purpose is all Laura's, though at that moment we aren't sure what that purpose is. Leigh is swept along, helpless and dreading what may happen. And the reader's interest remains high. Strong purpose *is* governing the scene, even though it's not Leigh's. However, it's best to use this device only when you can make it effective and dramatic. If the hero or heroine must be an observer temporarily, make sure there is deep emotional involvement in what is happening. Much must hang in the balance for your main character, so that what other characters do in such a scene critically affects him or her.

As you read fiction, watch especially how purpose is treated. Too often in a scene that drags, you will find there is nothing the main character is *attempting to resolve.* In a scene in which interest is high, you usually find that such an attempt is being made by the main character.

Problem, Purpose, Conflict, Goal—all build interest and suspense. Think about them as you plan your novel, and keep these elements at the back of your mind while you write. When you come to revise, check to make sure all four have been included in every chapter, in nearly every scene. If you omit any one, the omission should be intentional, and you should understand why you are leaving out one element or another.

Before we leave the subject of suspense, a word

should be said about clues and plants. They can be present in novels other than mysteries. The detective novel of the past presented the reader with a great many "clues"—false and otherwise. Later the detective or main character would add up these clues and try to figure out where they led. For me this always held up the story action, while nothing at all happened.

Today, when the mystery novel is turning in the direction of the psychological, with less emphasis on the formal puzzle, there are fewer standard "clues." (The dropped handkerchief with a telltale initial; the spilled perfume that points to a certain person; the impress of writing on a scratch pad, though the sheet has been removed.) However, there can still be red herrings (false clues) and plants. The misleading of the reader is still a major intent of the mystery writer, and readers of this genre like to be surprised and fooled.

Misdirection is (and should be) subtle. You want the reader to suspect everyone but the villain, so you may have an innocent character behave in a suspicious way. (Red herring again.) What he does, however, must be logical and eventually explained if you are to play fair.

The plant is something a little different. It is an honest indication that something in the story will be used again. Though you don't want the reader to guess this at the time. In *Vermilion* I introduced a macabre cane with a dragon's head. It is brought in as a murder weapon early in the story. However, since I meant to use it again, it is introduced into the action in rather an innocent way. The little girl, Marilla, brings it to the heroine as a malicious "gift." This is a justified scene, not something extraneous. The heroine puts the cane away in a closet—where it will be handy for use later on in the story. (The experienced mystery reader may say, "Ah-ha, a plant!" but it doesn't matter a lot, since he won't know how I mean to use the cane again.)

Plants are made so that the reader isn't suddenly surprised by the introduction of some object or fact that he's never heard of before, and thus won't believe in when it appears fortuitously.

The building of suspense is as endlessly fascinating to the writer as to the reader, and it isn't accidental. If there's a bit of duelling involved, then sharpen your weapons and become acquainted with their use!

9

SURPRISE YOUR READER

In *Suspense* the reader can often guess what will happen, but he doesn't know *how* it will come about, or how it can be avoided. He is in league with the character whom he wants to see escape disaster, or achieve some goal, but how this is accomplished is not revealed until the end of the scene, or even later.

Surprise, though related to suspense, is something the reader doesn't expect, or suspect. Sometimes that may even be true of writers, since we are happiest when we can surprise ourselves—and thus our readers.

You need both continuing suspense, and occasional surprises in your novel, but it is important to understand the difference between them.

While surprise is the stock-in-trade of the mystery writer, and accounts in part for the popularity of mystery and suspense novels, it is a valuable element in any sort of fiction, short or long. There are numerous methods by which you can stir up surprises and set your own imagination turning in unlooked-for directions that will heighten reader interest.

A reader who can anticipate what is going to happen is a bored and disappointed reader. When no one is jolted, editors yawn and send the manuscript back.

To achieve surprise, it's usually necessary for the writer to reject the first quick ideas that come to him in his planning stage. We've usually met these initial ideas so many times before that they are shopworn, and we need to reach back farther and deeper, where fresh items lie in hiding. Or, if the tired, overused idea is exactly what we want—which can happen on occasion—then we must give it a twist, or change it so it will seem new and exciting.

In my novel, *Domino,* for example, I used a room that had been locked up for years after a tragedy. I'd met that room in so many stories that I didn't want to use it. But since it logically existed in the setting I was writing about, it was just the plot device I needed. So I decided to make *my* room different. There is a closed mahogany box in the room. My heroine's desperate need to know what is in that box so whets the reader's curiosity that the cliché of a locked room doesn't matter. Of course, what is in the box is a total surprise, though pertinent to the story, and the reader won't guess what it is until I'm ready to reveal the secret.

Characters should always be your first source when you are looking for surprises. Even a character whose responses seem obvious can behave in an unpredictable way if you have planted the right traits to begin with. There can be seething emotion beneath the veneer of some outwardly calm character, and when it erupts, the unexpected will happen.

One effective device is to make your readers want to know the reason for a character's behavior. Then you postpone providing the answer. When you hint and hold back, curiosity is aroused, and a reader will put up with a good deal to find out the answers. This must not be done too often, however, or what is tantalizing can become merely annoying. This is not the same as stopping in the middle of a suspenseful scene and switching to something else in the next chapter.

In the planning stage, I make sure that all my characters have secrets that will be revealed gradually during the course of the novel. Such secrets will motivate all sorts of unexpected action and furnish the surprise element that I'm trying for. Before I ever get to the writing, I examine my characters for those secrets they may be hiding, and I plan ways in which such secrets may affect the lives of other characters in the story. Secrets make a wonderful source to draw on for the element of surprise.

Unexpected contrasts are also important. A character may enter a room and find surprises that reveal unexpected facets of the person who uses that room. Given a stereotyped character like "the stodgy businessman," the reader may observe on a table in his home an exquisite and imaginative piece of sculpture that he has created. A whole new and unforeseen light is cast on his character. Contrasts in behavior, in surroundings, in reactions, can offer an inexhaustible fund of surprising plot material.

"Had I but known . . ." is a phrase that is anathema these days. It began to be beaten to death in Mary Roberts Rinehart's day. Nevertheless, you'll be amazed (once you watch for it) to see how many modern versions of this old device are used today.

I've touched on "plants" in the last chapter. Forecasting, or foreshadowing, is more of the same—but different. What is planted when we foreshadow is anxiety. In the *Vermilion* example, the reader thinks nothing of the child's bringing the cane to the heroine. When we foreshadow, we deliberately arouse anticipation and a sense of approaching disaster. It is an excellent method for sustaining reader interest and promising surprises to come when the action has turned slow.

There are a great many ways to accomplish such foreshadowing. *There was a deathly quiet all through the house, but I knew that before I reached the next doorway.* . . . Or, the first person viewpoint character can ask herself a question to which she has no answer at the time. But since she is presumably looking back as she tells her story, she can hint at something fearful. Hint and hold out. But when the answer does come, make sure it is significant, so that the reader will feel rewarded. Above all, don't overdo this, or your readers will tire of the "trick" and become irritated with you as the writer.

The omniscient author, on the other hand, can do the same thing since the story is being told in third person and from several points of view. When I read M. M. Kaye's *The Far Pavilion* (a book that is a fine illustration of the successful handling of emotion, action, excitement, sympathetic characterization, etc.), I marveled at how often the author from her omniscient viewpoint played variations on the had-I-but-known theme. The promise of events to come that keeps readers reading is extremely effective.

It is not only the characters in a novel or story who can provide satisfying surprises. A place, a house, a room, a garden, can be filled with unforeseen possibilities.

The imaginative use of objects is always worth considering. Anything will do, provided the article is made important and significant to the characters. In *Poinciana*, when I introduced the collection of Japanese netsuke, I have a character say, "I had no idea how important these little carvings were to become in my life—or how disturbing." There is the had-I-but-known, the forecasting of disaster to come, with the focus this time on an object. One particular netsuke that I called "the Sleeping Mermaid," is of special importance and is used several times in the story, generating mystery and surprise.

In *Vermilion*, the ebony cane with an ivory dragon's head becomes almost a character in itself during the course of the story—so much so that the publishers decided to use the cane alone in a dramatic photograph for the jacket.

In the mystery novel, the big surprise is the twist at the end, when the writer presents the reader with an outcome he never expected. Because you have directed his attention elsewhere (like any skillful magician), he has not suspected the guilty person, or the secret answer. Or if he has, you have caused him to reject his own suspicions somewhere along the way. You have been able to mislead him through very hard work and the use of cleverness and skill. The cliché is true. Easy reading often means very hard writing. The writer plays a game with the reader, and oddly enough the reader likes it best when the writer wins and the reader is fooled.

Sometimes, of course, to relieve the conscious thinking through, there are also those gifts of inspiration that come surely and inevitably to every writer who is sufficiently immersed in his work and open to the lightning bolt. We can't command it to strike, though we can encourage it, but we must be ready and alert when it happens. Some of the best effects I've achieved in my writing have come to me through just such flashes of "inspiration." The Force at work again.

Perhaps my most dramatic surprise is achieved in the climax scene of *The Glass Flame*. In order to explain, I'm going to do what no proper mystery writer (or magician) ever does: I'm going to give away some secrets. However, if you haven't read the book and happen to do so now, you will read it with the special interest of a writer watching the legerdemain, and I won't lose you as a reader, even if you do know the surprise ending. Besides, I won't tell you *exactly* how it happens in the end!

Karen, my heroine, is married to a man named David. Shortly before the story begins, she has received a letter from him that says in part: "If anything happens to me down here, don't let it pass as an accident." (It has been fascinating to me that in the advertising for the book, and in the reviews, these words were nearly always quoted.)

I prepared the reader at once for David's death. If the reader isn't convinced in the course of the novel that David really is dead, I will fail in my moment of big surprise. With most readers, I apparently did not fail. A great many have written to tell me that when David walks onstage in all his villainy in the climax scene, very much alive, the reader's astonishment is complete. I've managed to saw the cabinet in two— and the "victim" emerges still intact!

It wasn't easy to accomplish this. From the first, I

knew I would be in trouble because I couldn't very well produce a body. And unless there is a bona fide body, any experienced mystery reader is going to say, "Ah ha! You can't fool me with those old bones. They might belong to anybody!" So I knew I had to convince my readers in spite of their better judgment. One of the comforting and reassuring things about writing is that there is always a way, always an answer. Sometimes it just takes awhile to discover what it is, and you simply keep on thinking and trying.

David's work was the tracking down of arsonists, and he had come to my setting in the Smoky Mountains to solve a problem of arson that faced his half brother, who is the real hero of the story. Thus it was perfectly appropriate for me to have David "die" in a fire. A body is found and presumed to be David's, but it is unrecognizable, because there has been an explosion as well as a fire.

Of course most readers become suspicious right there. *An unrecognizable body? What are you trying to pull?* I did furnish some evidence that it was David. He was known to have gone into the house; certain indestructible items of clothing are found that belonged to him—a belt buckle, etc. Not conclusive. The best I could do to overcome the lingering suspicions of my reader, was to have some teeth found in the ashes. David's dentist identifies them, and I skim delicately over the fact that only a bridge is found. I've been surprised that many readers apparently accepted this flimsy trick and took the bait right there, convinced that David was really dead. At this point, the mystery buff knows better. All the characters believe it, of course, but they can't be as smart or as suspicious of authors as mystery readers are!

From then on, it was my job—along with telling what I hoped would be a good story—to convince the reader that David was really dead. I think I did pretty well with this, but I wasn't satisfied. The book was three-quarters written, and I was still uncomfortably aware that some readers would see through my deception.

My unconscious had been fed the problem and told to come up with a convincing answer, but it was still slumbering. The lightning bolt, when it strikes, doesn't come out of the sky. It comes from within. My metaphor is wrong. It's more like an inner explosion that suddenly illumines the scene.

It came just in time, and I saw a very tricky way in which I could produce a body and make the reader believe it was David's. I could use the man who was really burned in the fire, but have his body discovered and mistaken for David *before* the explosion occurred. This necessitated the writing in of new scenes, but I always find it rewarding to do this extra work when I can see how much more effective it will make a story. At this point something already in the story suggested itself. The voracious kudzu vine of the South was almost a character in its own right, and now I saw an even more dramatic and eerie way to use it in scenes of terror connected with the finding of the body.

The reader now becomes convinced that David was murdered *before* he was put into the empty house that was to explode and burn. A small boy, who is a prominent character in the story, has found the body in a deserted shack overgrown with kudzu vines, and has "recognized" it as David. For a time, however, he has kept this knowledge to himself for his own very good reasons.

This was fine, as far as it went. I was still afraid that my readers would see that the identification was only partial and that a small boy could be mistaken. So I provided still another identification, this time by a woman (who has been fooled in the same way and kept silent because she is afraid the murderer is her husband). This apparently did the trick. Most readers never caught me at my sleight-of-hand, and even the diehards among them decided that David couldn't possibly be alive! There are such good reasons (provided by the sneaky author) to believe that the body is David's, without the final bit of looking into a bloody face—something that neither the boy nor the woman does.

As the reader approaches the climax scene, he is confounded when David, very much alive, walks in on my terrified heroine. I was pleased because things seldom turn out so well. I had worked very hard to achieve this and to find the surprise that satisfies my readers at the end of *The Glass Flame*.

This is one of the most useful things to remember about *Surprise*—it satisfies the reader.

10

SPRINGBOARD TO
FICTION
Where It Happens

There is one question that is always asked of the professional writer by the layman, and it comes so often that those of us who write automatically wince when we hear it. The question, of course, is, "Where do you get your ideas?" It's not that it isn't a legitimate question, but that the answer seems both so obvious and so complicated that it's hard to answer.

The simple and obvious answer is "Everywhere," but such an answer sends the questioner away as mystified as ever. Since those who don't write fiction never think they have any ideas for stories, there seems a magic in the way a complicated novel starts from nothing—and appears as a whole in a printed book.

It is the complicated part of that answer that I would like to discuss here. There are many, many times when the writer has no ideas at all, when he must start without any initial inspiration, and needs a springboard to launch him into that first idea. As he continues to work, other ideas keep attaching themselves to that initial one, until hundreds of manuscript pages have been filled, and the novel is completed.

A plot for a novel is not something that appears fullblown, as can sometimes happen with a short story. Actually, it is something that grows painstakingly and is nurtured by the writer from idea to finished manuscript. It grows a bit at a time, often after a writer goes through periods of despair.

My own special springboard is usually a new setting. The value of an interesting background, as I've suggested elsewhere, is something I learned early in my career as a fiction writer, and I learned by doing the wrong thing first.

Although I had lived in Japan, China, and the Philippines until I was fifteen, I was making up stories about the New York theater world, about Hollywood, and various other places I knew nothing about, but which sounded glamorous to me. Somewhere along the way, I stumbled on the earliest advice given the young writer: *Write about what you know.* Such advice usually seems boring to the beginner, and it didn't appeal to me at all. Who wanted to write about everyday happenings like earthquakes, typhoons, a jungle fire I'd seen, or about riding around in rickshas and traveling by boat up the Yangtze River—all that dull, prosaic material—when America was so interesting and different and exciting.

But I was willing to try anything to get published, so I finally wrote a story about that fire near a pineapple plantation where I'd lived in the Philippines. It sold, and I thought I was on my way. However, I soon found that I knew the Orient only through a child's eyes, and memories dimmed very quickly. What could I write about that *I* knew?

I had to find a new approach, still based on the fact that my imagination responded with enthusiasm and creativity to intriguing, unusual settings, and based also on the fact that I didn't really know any such settings. So I came upon the next rule: *If you don't know, find out.* And this rule has served me well ever since.

Any type of work, of career that I might investigate was sure to have its own background and special problems. Such backgrounds were, I found, welcomed by the magazines I was trying to reach. I could now write about Chicago by breaking the city down into segments that were small enough to handle.

I was not a very good short story writer. It was difficult for me to keep thinking up new ideas, and they wouldn't come as frequently as I needed them. Of the three hundred or more stories that I wrote during this period, I sold fewer than a hundred. During the Depression I tried a teen-age novel, although everyone told me this wasn't a good time to sell a book. In fact, I've been hearing that all my life. Right now (whenever "right now" is) we are being told that the market is very tight and that it is difficult for the beginner to get published. This has probably always been true. Mediocre stories are hard to sell. Really good stories are in demand. There are all kinds of markets out there, and one of them can be for you.

Against advice—because I *wanted* to—I wrote my first teen-age novel. It too was a "job" story concerning a group of young people who got together to provide services to the community in order to earn money. The idea grew from an article I'd read on this subject. Two publishing houses rejected the manuscript—the third accepted it, and *A Place for Ann* was published "in the worst of all possible times." I've been writing books ever since.

In writing for teen-agers I continued to combine jobs and local backgrounds for a while, until eventually I could move into other areas, even into foreign countries, and I no longer specialized in career stories only. New settings in themselves gave me story ideas and kept my imagination working.

Once I had a good background for a novel, I could set a human situation in a place that was fresh and exciting to me, and the plot and characters would begin to develop. The backdrop I chose would affect the characters and they would play their roles in particular ways within that setting, and would react in a certain way because of it.

All of this takes work and time. Though not as much as you might expect, once you have a plan. Not long ago a woman asked me a bit plaintively how I could spend a month in Turkey and Greece and come up with four books. Part of the answer is that by now I'm a good reporter, and I know ahead of time what I'm going after. I can offer a few specifics to others who may want to use this method of moving from background to story ideas.

First, I read as much as I can about the place I'm going to visit, and out of this reading comes a richness of ideas—always more than I can use. When I knew that I was going to both Turkey and Greece on the same trip, the first thing I did was to narrow my sights. A trip that takes in a whole country (or several countries!) in a short time results only in confusion. So when I went to Turkey, I decided upon Istanbul as the background for both an adult suspense novel and a juvenile mystery. In Greece, I chose the Isle of Rhodes as having wonderful possibilities, being off the beaten path from most popular writing about Greece. Again, I could write both a juvenile and an adult novel using Rhodes as the setting. In my advance reading, I concentrated on Istanbul and Rhodes.

I always use the viewpoint of a stranger coming into the special setting, since that viewpoint is closest to my own, and I can feel comfortable with it. My fictional stranger learns a great deal more than the average tourist because he is learning what *I* am learning.

Again, I return to my rule about breaking a setting down into small parts. I couldn't cover all the mosques in Istanbul, even if I wanted to, so I chose the Blue Mosque; I visited the Covered Bazaar; I discovered a picturesque fortress on the Bosporus that gave me some marvelous scenes. There was a small village nearby that I could use, and added to all this were city streets and the activities around Galata Bridge. Even my hotel was useful. I never rush about trying to see all the "sights" I can cover, but during my stay I keep returning to the few special places I've selected, until I feel I know them well. I can walk about in them in my memory and recall just how they smell and look and sound and feel. Of course I talk to anyone I can, and ask endless questions.

Notes go into a small, handy notebook that I index when I get home, so that any scrap of information can be quickly found. I set down facts, but even more I write my impressions. I've been asked why I don't use a tape recorder, and my answer is that I can't find what I want quickly on a tape, and it takes too much time to play it back. I would have to transcribe it anyway. A notebook, with a later indexing by subjects, is much more efficient, and when I need to find something I can do so in a hurry.

Of course I collect travel literature wherever possible, and search the bookstores for English-language books about the place I'm visiting. Often I find photographic collections that can't be obtained at home. I also take numerous color snapshots of anything and everything. I want to know how the streets and houses and people look. I buy the major scenes on postcards, which are nearly always available. Everything is of value to me—a springboard to ideas when it is all spread out on my desk at home and I go to work.

I use the same method for my research of places new to me in this country, and it works equally well, if not a little better, since there is no language problem. What is harder to accomplish is meeting the people who live in the area I want to write about. The manner of life varies from place to place. Architecture of homes is different, and so are the furnishings. I need to get *inside.* If I persist in asking for introductions, I am eventually welcomed into private homes. If I can visit several of these, I can later build my own fictional houses from bits and pieces, and have them true to the local scene I'm writing about.

I try to avoid professional guides and tours on my trips. How can I feel emotionally stunned by the Parthenon with a guide's canned chatter in my ear? Facts can be learned from reading. What I want most of all is *feeling.* There is a scene in both my books set in Rhodes, where the heroine sits on a stone wall in the sun in the ancient ruins of Camiros—and I think the reader will feel those scenes, because I sat in that exact spot and gave myself over to dreaming.

Wherever you go for new settings abroad, try to talk to new residents who are Americans. Newcomers in a country (who can speak your language) will have a keen eye for what is different and wonderful, or what is uncomfortable and disturbing.

For me, the background of my proposed novel must always come early in the development of the story. Though this isn't necessarily the very first springboard. Earlier germinal ideas can spring from nowhere, and sometimes lead me to a stimulating new setting.

The Stone Bull, title and all, came from a dream I had. I don't usually remember my dreams, but I woke up with this one vividly in mind. I had been wandering on a mountainside, on which appeared a huge barn. The door was locked, but I went in anyway, as one does in dreams, to find a very strange scene. I was in a bullring, with a large *stone* bull standing in the center of the ring. Here was a mystery with no answer, because I woke up immediately with just one thought in mind: *What a wonderful title for a book!*

Starting with the title alone, I had to find my mountainside. An editor wrote me about the Mohonk Mountain House near New Paltz, on the edge of the Catskills. I couldn't have found a more glamorous and romantic setting than this enormous Victorian hotel on a lake, surrounded by woods and hills. A place born for mystery!

Mohonk Mountain House cooperated in helping me get my background, and now *The Stone Bull* sells regularly in the hotel store. Guests even go out on the trails with my book in hand, looking for the places described in the story. I'm sure if I ever go back myself, I will find my stone bull waiting for me in its woodsy clearing.

But what of the times when you can't travel to distant parts? It doesn't matter. Settings are to be found anywhere. I've utilized every place I've ever lived in during my adult life, and some places I've only stepped into. Several of my books are set in Staten Island and in New Jersey, because I've lived in both areas. Once I wrote a book set in the United Nations building because someone suggested that a U.N. guide would make a good heroine for a teen-age novel.

Of course there may also be the times when you can't take even a short trip and you've "used up" that setting outside your window. What then? Phase Three —which I use every now and then with just as much satisfaction and enjoyment as I do the other two: I make it all up. That requires research, too. It needn't come entirely out of your head. There are always libraries and bookstores.

Before writing *Spindrift*, I had planned to go to Newport, Rhode Island, but had to cancel my trip. I was able to find a volume of splendid Newport photographs, and I pored over the pictures and text so many times that I could walk about the city in my imagination. I obtained a mass of booklets, brochures, maps, and other literature from the Newport Chamber of Commerce. Chambers of Commerce are always good sources of information about any American city or area. Libraries can be very helpful too. Through the Newport Library I found a woman who knew the city well, and who agreed to read my manuscript and to check it for accuracy. I would write to say that my character was in such-and-such a spot, and ask what she would see from that point if she looked out toward the water. Later this woman, who became a friend, read the entire manuscript to catch any mistakes.

This checking is necessary, even when I have actually visited a place. In spite of all my research it is easy to make simple mistakes that those who live in a place recognize at once. I am always annoyed when I read a novel set in the Orient and find the author referring to a hurricane. In the Far East the storms are always "typhoons." It is the small mistake you don't even know you are making that gives you away. Authenticity is all important.

Sometimes you make up a lot of the setting, even when you're writing about a real place that you've visited. When I was writing *Poinciana,* I found that I would quickly exhaust the outdoor Palm Beach background, so the house itself—Poinciana—is one of the important characters in the book. I took off in my imagination from a real and famous house—*Mar-a-Lago,* built by Marjorie Merryweather Post early in the century. Reality is often the springboard that takes me into an imaginary world. From then on, I let my setting grow however I please. I make diagrams and plans, so that I know the location of rooms I mean to use. I place them where I want and furnish them as I like, quite free of the original house that started me off. A real location must be accurately portrayed, if you name it, but within its boundaries you can take all the fictional liberties you wish. Sometimes, of course, it's fascinating to invent a whole city or town—and I've done that, too.

Before I leave the subject of setting, there are a few suggestions I'd like to make concerning the use of background in your stories. There is a richness of fabric when the reader can feel that he is walking around with the characters in the place where action is happening. This is where you will employ all your senses in description: sight, hearing, smell, taste, and touch. I'll talk about the use of sensory detail when we discuss emotion, but consider them now in connection with your settings. And don't forget them while you write.

Nevertheless, don't *clutter.* Too much detail can destroy the very picture you want to create. Everything should be clear in your own mind, but don't try to put it all into each scene. Weave it in with a few telling touches, and let your readers use their own imaginations.

Starting with a setting is only one of many possible ways to get into your story or novel. Use whatever method works for you; that stimulates your imagination. This won't necessarily be the same for every book you write. Somewhere along the way, however, whether you start with it or not, your background, your setting, will be important to your story.

11

Characters or Counterfeits

One of the most common faults to be found in the beginning writer's manuscript is that of poor characterization. Poorly drawn story people have names; they have eyes, hair, feet, hands; they are tall or short, thin or fat, and they talk and go through various motions. But they have about as much resemblance to living human beings as do cookie cutouts. Lacking life, they move the reader to no emotion and leave him uninvolved. If the manuscript comes back from an editor with the comment, "work on your characters," the young writer says in bewilderment, "How do I go about it?"

If you want to write fiction, you must, of course, have some understanding of human beings. Without understanding, sympathy, insight, empathy for others, no storyteller can get very far. You must *care* about other people if you are to make your readers care about your characters.

If you have a natural understanding of what motivates people, that's fine. Or you can read what appeals to you in the field of psychology—provided you avoid picking up the jargon.

The next requirement is a knowledge of how to go about creating real characters.

After I have my setting, I look next for a situation that will involve one or more characters. For years I have collected such situations. They can come from real life, from my reading, from anything. Before I finish my current novel, I feed such a situation into my mind, where it will have time to grow and collect a few ideas around it.

Starting ideas need be no more than a sentence in length: "A woman marries the man who was in love with her dead sister." That became *The Stone Bull.* "A girl who has a gap in her memory because of something terrible that happened in the past, must find the missing pieces." This turned into *Domino.* "A young woman marries a wealthy man and becomes stepmother to a girl nearly her own age,"—a situation that led to *Poinciana.*

A great deal of variety is possible using the same beginning situations. Sometimes I've even used the same ones for totally different books.

Such starting circumstances automatically present me with a character or two who faces a serious problem. Relationships barely hinted at set my imagination working, and I begin to think of the people who will populate my story. Whatever I find will be entered in the *Character* section of my notebook and allowed to grow.

Choosing a viewpoint character is easy for me, but may not be so in the story or novel you plan to write.

Sometimes you will choose the wrong character and need to change. Don't be afraid to experiment if something isn't working.

These days I prefer first person for my particular type of writing, though I began by using third person. For me, a first person narrative gives greater immediacy and urgency, a sense of more imminent danger. Also, when I use the first-person viewpoint, I don't have to worry about shifting from one character to another and breaking tension. In a short story, it is probably wise to use a single viewpoint all the way through, whether first person or third. In a novel, you may use several viewpoints if you choose, and if you feel more comfortable with a multi-viewpoint narrative. There are advantages and disadvantages to either method.

Your single viewpoint story can describe only what the main character sees, hears, experiences. Offstage action can be learned only through the words of another character: The viewpoint person *must* be in the scene you are describing. I find that the continuity, the ease with which the reader can follow the main character from scene to scene, the lack of confusion, is worth making a few sacrifices for. However, the invention of action may come harder for the writer when using a single viewpoint.

There are certainly stories that cannot be told from the single viewpoint. It may be necessary to get into the minds and action of more than one character. You can avoid annoying readers with viewpoint breaks by making the shift to a new viewpoint depict such exciting events that the reader is quickly caught up and carried along.

Avoid shifting viewpoints on the same page. Skipping back and forth into different characters can annoy the reader and be distracting. One viewpoint per chapter is usually advisable, though you'll find writers who won't adhere to this rule. When you're reading, test such skipping of viewpoint for what it may do to you as a reader.

Another danger in breaking viewpoint is that you may weaken suspense by telling too much when you get inside too many characters. All these elements must be weighed before you find the course that seems right for your story.

One special warning: Never write from the viewpoint of "they." This fault appears often in beginners' manuscripts. If you catch yourself writing, "they thought," "they watched," "they felt," get back into the single viewpoint of a "he," "she," or "I," as quickly as you can. The reader can feel nothing, nor can he identify with a multiple person.

Once I have named my characters, have some notion about the story situation, and know who the viewpoint character is, I begin work on my detailed character sketches. A collection of traits with physical attributes attached does not add up to a believable character. If you set down the word "jealous" in your description, you haven't created a jealous person until you know all about what motivates the jealousy, why it occurred in the first place, what direction it takes, what effect it has, what the character does about it, and so on. Unless you ask yourself the right questions, your character won't turn into a human being.

Here are the first two paragraphs I wrote about the heroine of *Poinciana:*

Sharon is blond, with long straight hair, wound in a knot at the back. Central part, with wings drawn away on each side. Large gray eyes with dark lashes. A beautiful figure and wears clothes well.

Outwardly calm and serene. Used to being relied upon by others. Used to doing as others wish. Yet beginning to resent this. Has an inward strength she is only just discovering. Never thinks of herself as beautiful. Wishes she looked like her piquant mother, who was a famous musical comedy star and much loved by Sharon's father. Grew up always taking second place to the demands of her mother's career, loving her father, but often impatient with him. Harbors resentments that she has never released, or faced in herself.

The sketch of Sharon goes on for five pages as she evolved gradually for *me*. As I talked about her on paper, I discovered what she thought of other characters in my story, and this began to bring them to life in my mind. *Knowing what each character thinks about all the other characters,* is an important part of the process. You are looking for feeling, *emotion*—and this must stem from your characters. Even the plotting, the development of story situations, will carry emotion only as your characters *react* to what happens and to the other people in your story.

As you write, questions about each character will evolve, and as you answer them, your story will grow. What problems face each one of your people? Why *must* these problems be solved? A problem that can be easily dismissed will take you nowhere. What does each character do? What are their professions, hobbies, hidden vices? What do they care about? Are they happy? What do they dislike? Inherent in your answers lies the emotion you are seeking, and the spark that will bring your people to life. As such questions are answered, ideas you never expected will come to light, and the characters will flesh out and move toward the day when they can step onto the stage of your story and be themselves.

There are still more questions. What is the *goal* of each one of your story people? I've mentioned "secrets" earlier. Now you ask yourself what secrets your characters keep from each other. At once whole new worlds of invention will open to you. In the actual writing, reveal these secrets gradually, so the reader feels there are always more surprises to come, and new things to find out about your characters.

Make sure that you don't make any of your characters either all good or all bad. Unless you can feel compassion for your villains, you won't be able to make them human. Why, you must ask yourself, does this dreadful person do such awful things? If you don't know what drives him—however far back in his past the reason may exist—he won't seem real to your reader.

Even your main character should have some faults. This can become tricky to accomplish, because if your protagonist isn't sympathetic, you won't hold your readers. (Unless you want the readers to hate the character so much that they keep reading to see him get his comeuppance. That can be satisfying too.)

When I begin a novel, I often have trouble making my main character sympathetic. She has serious problems, and sometimes she whines about them, or behaves badly. After considerable work, I make

changes so that in the end, she turns out to be the
admirable person I intended.

I like to give my heroines strong, individualized ob-
sessions or fears, because these create tension. And
tension builds interest.

There are a great many things to be afraid of in life,
and fear is one of the major emotions your main character will feel—not necessarily physical fear, though
there can be some of that. Fear builds tension that
leads to action, and the cause of fear may change in
the course of your story. If a character is afraid of
something in Chapter One, still afraid of the same
thing without any change in Chapters Two and Three,
the tension slackens. If the reader sees the character
express the same fear over and over again, the suspense ebbs and the reader is bored. Fear must grow
and change and turn in different directions, and so
must your characters. In the course of your story,
make sure the main characters either grow or deteriorate. A story is about change.

To help me visualize my story people and make
them real for me, I use certain devices. If you think of
a woman in your story as resembling some current
movie star, that's fine—but don't tell the reader. This
is a lazy substitute for real characterization, and it
becomes tiresome through repetition by writers who
ought to know better. When a writer tells me that a
character looks like a famous actor, I am confused. In
my imagination I see the actor instead of the fictional
character. You can use characteristics of famous people if you like, but you must still develop and shape
them more fully into characters that are your own
creation.

Sometimes I clip pictures of interesting faces out of

papers and magazines—usually of people I know nothing about—and use them to help me "picture" my characters. You can find good faces in advertisements, fashion catalogues, or magazines. It is very hard to describe a face, because you must not try to give all the details; a few highlights will usually suffice.

I can't use people I know as characters in my novels, because their real-life roles would get in my way. Some writers may draw their characters from friends and acquaintances, but that is not my method. Of course I constantly collect bits and pieces from everyone I see or know, though I no longer do this deliberately and often don't remember where some detail came from that I find useful.

Television plays and advertising can be a great source of fictional people when you are creating your characters. You can stare without being caught. Also, actors are versed in revealing character in small movements and gestures that a writer too can learn.

I find it helpful to go through my thesaurus to collect a few adjectives, adverbs, and verbs that accurately describe each character. I do this *after* I've worked out each role, so this is not a substitute for characterization, but helps me to visualize my people more clearly.

Sometimes, when a character won't come to life, in spite of all the work you've done, set him at your typewriter and tell him to start a diary. As he begins to talk about himself in the first person, a spark is likely to kindle, and suddenly there is life where previously there was only a collection of words. You may be surprised to learn what he thinks of the others in your story, or maybe even of *you*—if you've been pushing him in the wrong direction. It's a good idea to listen to what your characters want to tell you.

When you finally bring your cast onstage to perform, make sure that each one reveals as soon as possible the sort of person he is by what he says and does, and in the case of your viewpoint character, what he is thinking. Not everything at once, of course. In writing a novel, you have room to introduce details more gradually than in a short story. It is never good enough to *tell* the reader, that is, to have one of your characters (or you as the author) explain that someone has a quick temper. This may be said, but you must also prove it. *Show, not tell,* is the first rule about writing that you need to learn. Here is a simple illustration:

Dorothy was the sort of woman who quickly resented any slight. Here I am *telling* you about Dorothy. I am standing between you and the action, so that it's my voice you hear.

Dorothy's eyes flashed, and with not the slightest warning she slapped the young man across the face. A little extreme, but the reader is convinced. This is showing, dramatizing. As author, I am invisible, and in today's writing that's the way authors should stay.

If you've done your preparation well, your characters will show life signs as soon as they walk onstage. The emotion will be felt immediately, though sometimes it may not take the form you expect.

In my novel *Vermilion,* I had pictured a nine-year-old girl. I knew a lot about her: She was an unhappy child, loving a mother who was indifferent to her, longing to be loved by a father who was often away. Consequently, she was a solemn, brooding child. Dark hair, dark eyes, a little malicious—I had her character all worked out, I thought. Then she skipped into a scene when I didn't even expect her! Her hair was a cap of short fair curls about her head, and she was filled with a lively curiosity, an openness, an interest in my main character that was disconcerting. There was still a trace of malice, which she needed, but I liked her much better and found her more interesting and useful to me than the child as I first saw her. She went her own way, and it was better than mine. Nevertheless, I kept an eye on her, because I suspected that she would demand center stage and start taking over, though it wasn't her story.

If a character shows signs of going off in a new direction, examine what is happening. Decide whether the changed course is likely to hinder or further your story. Will it take you down some side road that you never wanted to travel? Sometimes it's difficult to decide, and the only thing you can do is to experiment for a few pages, or for a chapter or two. By that time you may have something more concrete to help you choose. If the new direction is a good one but means making changes in what you have already written, don't worry. You can always go back and build in the new elements. Nothing you set on paper is in concrete!

Animals as well as children can be useful in your stories. But they must never be there only for trimming. They must *belong.* An animal can become a real character in your story and serve the plot. Readers enjoy interesting creatures of all kinds. In *Domino,* I have a dog, Red, who plays an important role in the plot's events. What he does affects the heroine's life, yet at the same time adds a touch of humor and emotion.

Another kind of character whom we mustn't overlook is the person who has died *before* the first chapter begins. Such a person can seem to be strongly "onstage" (in memory or flashback) and will serve us well, even to the extent of generating much of the current action. Ariel, the heroine's ballet-dancing sister in *The Stone Bull,* is just such a character. Though she has died shortly before the novel opens, the story would collapse without her. In *Vermilion,* Jed, the heroine's father, is an equally important character, and even though the reader knows in the first sentence that he's dead, he becomes as real as if he were onstage throughout the story. What he was affects several characters and influences the story action. Again, the novel would collapse without him.

In fact, this is probably a good test of any element in your novel. Will the story fall apart if you take it out? If not, it's just an adornment. You may have enjoyed writing it, but it may not belong.

These techniques of character development are intended to help your fictional people come to life. There is a sort of magic that emerges, if we feed enough good material into the unconscious. It is this magic that will eventually flow from your fingertips as you write, and bring to life the people you are writing about and make them memorable.

12

THE SATISFYING
ELEMENT
Emotion

Emotional impact is one of the most vital—and often most neglected elements in fiction. It is important, not only when it relates to what characters feel about themselves and one another, but in the emotional reaction and response they must arouse in readers to make them accept what the writer is saying— *and care about what is happening.*

How do you put your finger on so intangible an element? Naming an emotion doesn't produce it: We can claim that our characters are angry, frightened, grieving, or whatever, but we do not thereby produce in the reader a feeling of anger, fright or grief. How then do we use this elusive quality effectively in our fiction? It can be done, it must be done, and there are some specific ways in which you can use it quite deliberately.

Emotion is the product of all the other elements that make up a successful piece of fiction writing. Let's consider first the obvious sources of emotion.

Feeling grows out of our characters, of course. Unless the story people come to life and express their emotions and reactions, there will be no feeling transmitted to the reader. Wooden characters produce no emotion, and there is nothing for a reader to experience.

The level of emotional response reflects the importance of the story problem. Is it a life-or-death matter to the main character? Perhaps not literally—though it may be that, too. In either case, happiness must hang in the balance. Will there be great rewards if the main character succeeds in attaining his heart's desire? Will there be real disaster if he fails? If the problem doesn't matter one way or another, the reader will feel little about characters or story.

There must be not only importance, but also a furious struggle—both inner and outer—otherwise, no emotion will result. No matter how serious the problem, if it is too easily resolved, no one will care, no one will feel anything. The author's effort to whip up emotion when none of what is happening really matters, is sure to result in the synthetic—which the reader will be quick to detect and will make him put the novel down.

Another source of emotion grows from a story's meaning. If the whole exercise is pointless, there is a vacuum of feeling. Even a well-drawn character engaged in a powerful struggle that lacks meaning—significance—will leave the reader saying "so what?"—and therefore unsatisfied.

With effort and practice, fiction writers can learn to

handle these means for evoking emotion in their readers, and to do it skillfully, there is still another factor
that must not be overlooked. Perhaps the word atmosphere covers it as well as any. By this I mean the way
everything around your characters becomes so real
that the reader reacts with feeling, just as your characters must. By "atmosphere" I don't mean setting
alone. Setting, to me, means physical background. Atmosphere indicates all the subtle emanations of emotion that can arise from the physical elements in your
story. It's not enough to set a mountain in front of the
main character. We need to know how he feels about
that particular mountain.

Fictional people don't move in empty space. Their
world, like ours, consists of sticks and stones, tables
and chairs, hot and cold, rough and smooth, loud and
soft, sour and sweet—all of which are conveyed
through our five senses and bring about emotional
reactions. In other words, these emotional responses
stem directly from the impressions the characters re-
ceive through their senses of sight, hearing, touch,
taste, and smell. How a character reacts to the mes-
sages he receives, is determined by (or is the result of)
his emotional response. This is the factor that the novice writer often forgets to reveal in his story: *How does
the character react?*

Emotion can be built from sensory responses even
when there is no strong character, important problem, or significant event. It won't be as intense an
emotion as it would be if these elements were present,
but it can exist in itself. The following illustration
shows what I mean: Let me take a "character" about
whom I know nothing—not his name, his problem, his
purpose—nothing. I don't even know how he looks.

But by setting him in motion and supplying a few sensory details, I can produce at least a mild emotion in the reader. See for yourself how it works here:

> A man gets off a train in the city in a rainstorm, and there is no one there to meet him. He leaves the drab gray area of the station and turns down a side street. It is late afternoon, but because of the storm, it has been dark for a while, and the street lights glimmer through the driving rain. Puddles of dirty water on the pavement throw back a dismal reflection. The rain is cold and he turns up the collar of his coat with fingers that feel stiff. Already the thin soles of his shoes are soaking through. A car flings up a careless arc of muddy water as it turns a corner, and he is not quick enough to avoid the splatter that soils his gray slacks.
>
> Along this narrow side street the few passersby are in a hurry and they are isolated by the small worlds of their own umbrellas. At windows high above, blinds have been pulled against the darkness and the rain, shutting him out.
>
> From a third floor window comes the laughter of a girl, high and clear. It is a sound he cannot share. If she met him now on the street, she would pass him by like the others. As he crosses an areaway, the smell of stew cooking drifts out to him and he sniffs the aroma hungrily. He fingers the few coins in his pocket, and they are clammy cold to his touch. A cup of strong hot coffee and a doughnut will have to do.

I haven't told you anything about this man. I have given you sensory details, plus a mood, and from these you have drawn a picture in your mind. If I had merely told you that the man was cold and lonely, you would have seen nothing, felt nothing. By using simple sensory details, plus *the emotional reaction of the character,* I have touched you just a little. This reaction by the character is so important that we can take exactly the same scene, using all the same sensory details, and change the entire effect merely by changing the man's *reaction* to them. This time I will italicize the words that show the emotional reaction of the character:

> A man gets off a train in the city. It is raining, and he *strikes out* down a side street with a *quick, strong* step. It is late afternoon, and he *likes* the way early street lights *shine* through the driving rain and *dance* in the puddles at his feet. The cold rain is *bracing, exhilarating,* and he *doesn't mind* the drop or two that go down his neck as he turns up his collar.
>
> People hurry along isolated by their own little umbrella worlds, and he *tries to glimpse* their faces as they pass. *Perhaps there are friends* to be found among these passersby.
>
> Up on a third floor he hears the *ringing* laughter of a girl, and his step *quickens.* He *could like* a girl who laughs as *wholeheartedly* as that. This street is *for him. Before long perhaps he'll find out who she is.*
>
> When he sniffs the *rich, savory* smell of stew cooking, he *doesn't hesitate.* He *runs* up the steps and *rings the bell.*

Here the sensory details are the same, but each of the men reacts to them in totally different ways: The mood is different, and thus a different emotion is built in the reader.

Once when I gave these two examples at a writers' conference, a member of the class commented on the fact that she felt the emotion in the first example to a greater degree than she did the opposite emotion in the second. The reason is simple. Even though we know nothing about either man, we sense that the first man has a problem. The second does not have one as yet. It is a simple rule that trouble (a problem) is a main ingredient required to produce interest in any story.

John Ciardi once said that words "cast an emotional vote." We must be aware of this constantly. If we are sensitive to this emotional quality of words and understand the reactions of each character in the story, we can produce in the reader whatever emotion we want him to feel. But first the elements to which he can respond *must* be included in our stories—all those elements covered by the word "atmosphere": setting, both indoors and out; time of day and of season, the weather, as well as the physical objects around us.

I have found it helpful to keep a "weather calendar." Some years ago I took an old engagement calendar with blank pages and began to make random entries. Some of my notes are simply a factual record of what blooms when, and how it looks.

An early April entry: *Fuzzy soft green of a leafing willow tree. The winter landscape softly smudged as if an artist had rubbed his thumb across it. Trees not yet leafing, but no longer hard and bare.*

There are entries made during a blizzard, a thunderstorm, on a very hot day, and so on. When need arises in a story, I can turn to any time of the year I please and find notations to help me recreate the scene in my story. In every such entry, emotion is inherent because I myself have seen, felt, *reacted*.

Such reaction on the part of our characters must go on constantly throughout each story or novel, but there is still another form of response which, if forgotten by the author, will result in a lack of emotion—and satisfaction—for the reader.

In the example of that walk in the rain, we were not deeply inside either man. There were few clues to the thoughts of either. But in order to build strong emotion in our stories, and thus in the reader, the writer must interweave the feelings of the main character throughout the action. This can be done by revealing his actual thoughts. If the reader doesn't know what the character is thinking and feeling about the story events, or about the other characters, the reader cannot possibly feel with him or through him.

In writing a novel or a short story, the writer takes the reader inside the mind of a character. Few other mediums accomplish this, yet beginning writers (and sometimes experienced ones) often fail to take advantage of this powerful device.

The following is an example from a beginner's story in which the character's reaction is so bland that there is no emotional impact for the reader. Here, the boy hero is running away to another town and well along on his course, he hears a sound behind him and turns to investigate. He finds that a little girl who is fond of him has followed him on his runaway journey and has fallen and hurt herself. He is (or should be) shocked, angry, worried, concerned. His plans are now spoiled because he is handicapped by his own sense of responsibility toward the younger child. But we have to guess at all this because the author tells us nothing as far as the hero's inner response is concerned. Here is the place where he has heard the sound and turned back:

> Quickly he climbed up to the spring. There, almost hidden by the boulders, was Ida. She was using her hands to drip water over a swollen ankle.
> "Ida, what are you doing here?" His voice was angry and loud . . .

The scene continues with dialogue, and the reader feels nothing of the dramatic emotional impact that should be present in this scene. We don't feel the boy's anger from *inside*. We don't know anything about his feelings and *inner* reactions. The fact that his voice is "angry and loud" is objective, not subjective information. This is only *naming* the emotion, not living it.

You must not allow emotion too full rein when you are trying to show what a character feels. Restraint is always a good watchword. The character who behaves like an old-fashioned actor emoting all over the stage is more apt to reduce the scene to the ridiculous, so that the reader squirms, and true feeling is destroyed. It is a good habit to play down our most dramatic scenes. The action in itself carries the drama, and major emotions are easily understood. Anger and grief and terror can be easily conveyed, and they will be all the more effective for being presented in a low key.

Fiction writers must also beware of cluttering their scenes with too much sensory detail. It takes only a few vivid phrases to build a scene. As human beings, we don't have time to react to every detail of what we see around us, and so our characters should not react to everything either. Select the most useful details, and the reader will fill in the rest for himself.

To make sure that *I* will get into the mood and feeling of a scene, I've found it useful to "rehearse" the opening action in my mind *before* I go to my typewriter. When I try to write a scene "cold," there is often a long warm-up period before I can actually get going. Or what I write is so wooden that it has to be done over the next day. I find that a few minutes taken in advance pays off in time saved later.

Before I start to write a new scene, I visualize the setting (wordlessly at first) and set my actors moving against it. I sit quietly and *watch* it happen in my mind. I *live* what is happening through the main character. Whatever feeling is inherent in the scene becomes part of me. When words of description and dialogue begin to come to me, it is usually time to write. When I can visualize successfully ahead of time, the scene works itself out with ease and fluency at my typewriter, and I am launched into my morning's work. If there is another sticking point, I simply repeat the process.

Another helpful device for creating the right emotional reaction in each scene is to set down a few key words ahead of time, just as you may write certain key words about the characters. You will already know the main emotional effect you want in the scene—that is, the primary emotional reaction of your main character. If he is to feel deep dejection, turn to your thesaurus and write down a few words by way of reminder: dejection, depression, oppression, disheartenment, drooping spirits, despondency, etc. You may need to use none of these in the writing, but because words carry that "emotional vote," by looking at them, *you* react, and you are less likely to let your main character show cheerful, happy thoughts at an inappropriate time in your novel.

If your writing has been of the "bare bones" variety —what one editor called "bare dormitory writing," meaning *unfurnished*— then it's also helpful to make a quick list of sensory details you might use in a particular scene. Think of the place in which the scene will be played, the time of year, the view outdoors, or from a window. A few key words will serve to remind you that there is a world out there, and that your main character needs to see, hear, taste, touch, smell, and *react to.*

Putting emotion into our writing, satisfying our readers, is no chance thing. However intangible emotion may be in itself, there is nothing intangible about the means of evoking it. If you are aware of the factors we've been discussing, if you yourself can feel the emotion, then your writing will leave readers satisfied. It will say something to them about human beings; it will entertain and hold them spellbound—it will make them *experience* your story happenings. They will come back to you for a repeat performance in your next novel.

13

FLASHBACKS, TRANSITIONS, AND TIME

All three of these elements are important in your fiction writing, and they can all give you trouble, unless you are aware of their uses and their pitfalls. All three are interconnected. Transitions occur at the beginning and end of a flashback, as well as in movement from scene to scene. Time is part of everything that happens in your story. However, in order to clarify, I'll deal with these elements separately, though the interrelationship should be kept in mind.

FLASHBACKS

You may find these confusing to handle. When should a flashback be used? How to move back and forth without losing reader interest? When should it be avoided altogether?

In writing a short story, the flashback should probably not be used, though there are exceptions to everything. In a novel, it may be necessary to turn back in order to dramatize long clumps of what would otherwise be dry exposition, or a dull "remembering." There is always information that needs to be imparted before the reader can fully understand what is happening, or has happened. It would be fine if we could plunge immediately into action and not stop for such explanations. Unfortunately, this is seldom possible. A great deal has happened to bring your characters to their present plight, and the reader can't follow your story until he understands something of this. There are always going to be the *Who, What, When, Where* and *Why* to consider. It is the more complicated *Why* that gives us trouble. A flashback can take the reader into an earlier scene, dramatizing the action as if it were happening onstage in the present, and so make the explanation and information more interesting. "Explaining" always needs to be held to a minimum.

Usually, a flashback will come near the beginning of a novel. It's possible to start with interesting action that makes all the other elements clear, pulling your reader along and making him curious. Once you have his interest, you can safely slip into a scene that has taken place before the story begins, and gradually return your reader to present happenings that carry the story ahead.

In my novel, *The Winter People*, I surprised myself with a type of flashback that I'd never used before, and really hadn't meant to use then. Here is the opening paragraph:

I was asleep, and then I was awake, listening. I could hear the snow hissing at the windows, hear the storm behind it and the rushing sound the wind made through the pine trees. But the sound that awakened me was inside the house. A key had been slipped into a lock.

This present action continues for about two and a half pages and is sure to capture the reader's interest. The heroine awakens to the sound of a key locking her in her bedroom. Her husband is gone from their bed, and a woman who hates her has locked her in. This is quickly obvious, and it is clear that the heroine is in a lonely house in the country, with a snowstorm coming up. But of course the reader doesn't know how this situation evolved. I hoped that the tantalizing events of the opening would make my readers curious enough to go along with an explanatory flashback that would follow.

Finding the right place to start a flashback is important. Don't stop in the middle of exciting action to have your character think back to previous events. Let your hero or heroine find a quiet time, when the situation may be difficult, but nothing *immediate* is happening. Otherwise you will annoy your reader. The perennial childhood question, "What happens *next?*" still needs to be answered for your readers. Tension has been built to a high point, and no reader likes to turn back or leap ahead at that moment.

The scene from *The Winter People* continues until my main character settles down beside the fire she has lighted in her bedroom and begins to think quietly through the events that have brought her to her present plight. This is the resting point at which a flashback to previous happenings can begin.

After a *little* exposition as Dina thinks back, I switch to something that had taken place in New York when she worked as assistant to the curator of a museum. Her future husband had walked into this scene, and I present it as if it were happening now. (Not, of course, in present tense.) The past perfect should be dropped quickly. A few "had's" establish past action, and then you continue with the simple past tense.

All I meant to do in this flashback scene was to present a chapter that would be set in New York and show through dramatization how Dina came to be in her present predicament. Instead, all these past happenings became so interesting, that I just kept on going through everything that had occurred, until I once more reached the moment when the key turned in Dina's door. On page 155!

This alarmed me, because I was obeying none of the flashback "rules." That is: Don't make your flashback too long; or if it continues for a while, return to the present scene now and then, in order to remind the reader that this *is* a flashback. Always make it very clear whether you are in the past or the present when you make a change. But I did none of this in *The Winter People.* I never pointed out again that this was a flashback. Nor did I mention it when I caught up with the opening scene and went on with it. The story simply continued. Whether it would work or not, I didn't know. But after the book was published there were no outcries, no confusion on the part of readers. They simply went along with the story and accepted what was happening.

That technique worked so well, that I tried it again in *Poinciana,* using a flashback that is nearly as long. I did no switching back and forth, but just went on with the story until I caught up to the place where I'd left my heroine in the library of Poinciana in the story opening.

On the other hand, flashbacks can be very unsettling to a reader. In writing *The Glass Flame,* there was a point at which I felt the action was going to be too slow, and I flashed *ahead* to more exciting happenings, and then went back to explain more briefly what had occurred earlier. When the manuscript was sent in, the weakness in this forward-and-back action was pointed out by several readers. I kept rewriting the transition points in an attempt to make everything clear. In the end, when the book was published, most readers accepted these scenes without any trouble, but I received a few indignant letters, including one from a woman who said that she thought there were some pages missing in the book because something had been skipped. (Readers won't always tell you what they like, but they never miss a chance to point out what's wrong!) In the long run, what I'd tried was not a good idea because I hadn't handled it properly.

The more orthodox back-and-forth technique can be very useful and effective, if you manage not to confuse the reader. In Stephen King's *Firestarter,* he opens the novel with father and small daughter on foot, being pursued by a green car on the streets of Manhattan. This hooks the reader right away. Then, when the present scene comes to a resting place, he switches back to some time before, when it all started, and dramatizes the past scene, giving us the action as it happened. But first he has made us very curious to know what it was that occurred in the past—which is the real secret of a successful flashback. Much of the first part of the book alternates between past and present stories, and both are kept suspenseful, so the reader is willing to leave one thread and pick up the other. King always makes it clear whether the action takes place in past or present. When the two finally coincide, the story moves ahead in the present to the end. This is all skillfully and effectively done and is worth studying for suspense—the building of high tension and anxiety.

The danger of the flashback lies in confusing your readers, and possibly losing their interest when you make the switch in time, either back or forward to the present. The reader becomes interested in the scene before him and doesn't want to be pulled away, so the new action, whether past or present, must be made arresting at once, with a new piece of action, serious conflicts or threats.

For the novice writer, it is probably safest to use the brief, early flashback, when necessary. Get your explaining over as quickly as you can by dramatizing past action, and then move on with the story people. However, there are no absolute rules about anything in writing, and if you want to experiment, do so. If it turns out badly, you can always do it over.

TRANSITIONS

When I need to write a transition scene, inspiration usually forsakes me. I know that it will be necessary to mark time before I go into the next interesting action. If I don't let the reader rest now and then and catch his breath, I may lose his interest. Fast action all the time can become monotonous, even if it could be made believable, and there can be a loss of the reader's interest.

In a novel, there are transitions of time, when hours, days, sometimes years must pass, and I often find such scenes hard to write. But I know they must be done painstakingly and without losing reader interest. If you find you've suddenly become bored with the book you're writing, notice whether you're in a transition passage, and take courage. *Your* interest will pick up when this tiresome spot is behind you.

There are also transitions of place, and these, too, require skill and patience. I often need to move my characters from here to there, but if I describe their movements every step of the way, it will clutter my story and put the reader to sleep. Don't write: *She left the taxi, crossed the sidewalk, climbed four steps and entered the vestibule, where she rang the bell.* There is a strong tendency to do this when you are visualizing every step of a scene sharply in your mind. Such transitions should usually be done quickly and clearly. Just get her there in a few words and let her ring the bell!

There is another type of transition that makes use of the passing of time. You can sometimes use an object to show the changing of the time of day, or even the time of year. Perhaps something as simple as a birdbath in a garden. Your character views it in early morning, the water shining in sunlight, birds busy around it. Then you show it again at night, with shadows darkening and the birds asleep, so that the reader knows time has passed. Or you can take the same birdbath from autumn, with dead leaves floating on the water, to a day when ice is forming.

In simple transitions it is wise to put the words that indicate a change in time or place at the beginning of a sentence or paragraph. Don't go on for some words or sentences and *then* indicate that it's the next day or a new scene. Readers are disconcerted when they aren't informed that a change has taken place.

However much you love to read—and all writers need to be addicted readers—you must learn to read *as a writer.* You are no longer a "tourist" as you read, amusing yourself. Now you live there. Enjoy the story, lose yourself in it, but keep your writer's eye open for how a technique is being handled by the writer. This is especially helpful for learning about transitions. In the next piece of fiction you pick up, notice how the author manages to move about in both time and place. If you find a transition especially skillful, make a note of the method used. Then, when the time comes, you can follow the same process. *Your* transition will be different, of course, but you'll learn the means used far more graphically if you analyze what happens in the stories and novels you read.

TIME

Time can be your ally, or it can be an adversary. It is an active factor in all fiction. At the very beginning of your story or novel, the reader must know what time of year it is, even what time of day—morning, afternoon, night. Sometimes even the exact hour is important. Or the exact year, if historical events are involved. In each new scene, the time of day must again be noted, and in transitions of either place or time, the reader must be aware of elapsed minutes, hours, days, years, as these apply.

There are various ways in which we can convey the passing of time unobtrusively. I've already touched on some of these under *Transitions.* There are additional devices we can use. Sometimes, when there is a time break within a chapter, we simply double space and start with a new scene in a way that tells the reader that a certain amount of time has passed. This method may save you the effort of writing a full transition if you use it judiciously. Overuse may give your writing a choppy effect.

One of the most effective (and easiest) places to put a time break or shift is between chapters. The danger here is that if you are building up to a point of high tension at the close of one chapter, and do not describe the action immediately in the opening of the next chapter to resolve the suspense, you may lose the tension you have created. For the reader, there is less of a sense of urgency when too much time passes, and he may reason that if the threat didn't materialize right away it probably never will. In most cases I prefer not to use this type of time break, since I like to build up tension and immediately resolve it.

However, there is another way. This is the closing paragraph at the end of one chapter in *Poinciana:*

> Anger began to stir in me again, but this time it was a quieter, stronger, more reasoned emotion. Tomorrow, somehow, the struggle must begin. It must begin with me.

This is a promise of something interesting to come. However, it doesn't leave the reader at a point of exciting action, thus unsettling him with a time leap in the next chapter, which begins:

> After a breakfast that Ross sent up to my room, I
> felt somewhat better. . . . The quiet anger with
> which I'd fallen asleep had not abated, but this
> morning I knew I must move with care. I mustn't
> flare out blindly against whatever threatened
> me.

There is continuation here of a quiet sort, and time
has been passed.

It is sometimes easier to show the passing of long
periods of time in stories by using third person. First
person is too often tied into immediate action. At the
beginning of a chapter, you may even step out of viewpoint and become omniscient. In my teen-age novel,
Step to the Music (written in third person), I was writing about happenings during the Civil War. Therefore,
the larger panorama of history was important, and I
found I could touch on this sometimes at the beginning of a chapter:

> Sunday, July 21, 1861, was the day of the picnic.
> It was also a day that would go down in history.
> Though the picnickers knew nothing of the fact,
> certain curious maneuverings were under way
> across the Potomac River.

I get back quickly to my characters, but the reader
has been made aware of the exact date, and of omi-
nous happenings away from the immediate scene;
events that will affect their lives.

There is another element of time that is important
in holding your reader. If the use of a time limit can be
worked in naturally, it's a very effective device for
creating suspense. Something *must* be accomplished

before such-and-such a time—or else! Disaster will strike at a particular time—day, hour, minute. High noon! Characters who must struggle, not only against an opponent, but against time itself, dramatically heighten story interest and suspense.

Immediacy is also an important element in a piece of fiction, but it is not easy to define or achieve. Though dictionaries agree that the word means "the quality of being immediate," what it means to me is that something is happening *right now*. The time element is the immediate present. None of those annoying "had's" that place action in the past and slow everything down. The reader wants dramatic action to happen *now*, as it does in any story in which the characters and setting come to life and make the reader feel he is on the scene, not only watching it happen, but taking part in the action. Immediacy is part of transitions, flashbacks, and all are aspects of time in fiction.

If you will think of the scene you are writing as though you are one of the actors, you'll achieve immediacy, and the "now" sense of time will work for you in your fiction writing. Transitions will flow more easily, the flashback will be conquered, and time will be your ally.

14

REVISIONS AND REWRITES

Sometimes I think a fiction writer must get a story or novel down on paper before he can discover his true direction. What you may have written—however badly—is never wasted. Seeing it in written form, however rough, will set you on a surer course.

When you first do these early drafts, you won't want to believe that you've written badly. We writers become intoxicated with our own words and can't bear to think there is anything wrong with them. We can read our own writing over and over with enthusiasm, pleasure and appreciation—only to be faced in the end with the grim realization that not all those beautiful words are so beautiful after all, and that we've been deluding ourselves.

As a writer, I learned early on how to take criticism. As a teacher of writing, I could distinguish at once between professional and amateur because the beginner always falls apart emotionally when a manuscript is criticized. He reacts with raw feelings, resents, disputes, and will argue all the way down the line. He hasn't learned yet that criticism must be accepted intellectually, and not with the emotions. There is really nothing personal about it. Nobody is saying that *you* are stupid, but only that you haven't done it properly yet. My characters can often behave in very stupid ways, before I catch on to what they're doing.

When you can accept the fact that revision is a necessary part of successful writing, you will be able to face it more philosophically and professionally. By this time, revision is the phase I enjoy most. First writing is sometimes a joy, when it catches fire, though often it can be painful and slow. But once it's all down, I can mold it into the shape I want.

No one except me could ever read one of my manuscripts in its rough state. I seldom write at such length that I have to cut. Instead, I tend to write my fiction too tightly, and must then insert and elaborate, deepen and expand. Nearly every page is penciled with corrections, and on the back of most pages I write in pencil the new material that will really make the book. To this day, I find that physically putting pencil to paper is another way to get that writing flow started. I can *think* with a pencil.

Now, when a fault is pointed out to me, I can see it for myself (though I couldn't before), and can start figuring out how to fix what is wrong. This part is fun— making it come out right. Remember: good books aren't written; they are rewritten. Revision is a key phase of your novel writing.

With short fiction pieces, it's advisable to put them

aside and let them "cool" for awhile. Only then can you go back to your own work with a fresh and somewhat objective eye and catch a few of your mistakes. Though you'll never see them all. Fortunately, with a novel, when you've written your way through the last chapter, enough time will have passed so that you can return to the beginning with more objectivity. Though even then *you* can't be entirely objective.

Here are a few questions to help you check your own work during revision. In a way, this entire book is a check list and can be used when you come to revise. However, this shorter list will help remind you of danger spots to watch for.

1.   Are the time and place of your action always clear? Not only in the opening scene, where it's very important to orient the reader, but all the way through. Especially at the beginning of a chapter or a new scene.
2.   Are your characters consistent in their behavior? This may be hard to achieve in the first drafts, when you'll lose track of what has happened earlier. Now you can watch for such detail as you read.
3.   Have you individualized your characters so that they aren't just types? Is this done all the way through? Although you won't give a full description every time an actor walks onstage, you do want to jog the reader's memory by repeating touches of description here and there. Readers like to visualize as the story continues.
4.   Have you given your settings some unique details that you refer to as the story goes on? Just because you've described a room or an outdoor scene at the beginning, don't count on having your

reader remember it later in the novel. Touch in a detail or two as a reminder, so that your story does not seem to move in a vacuum.

5.   Are there any characters onstage that you've forgotten about and left standing around without anything to do or say? If you don't need them, get them off! If you do, use them, so the reader won't wonder what's happened to so-and-so.

6.   Does your main character have a strong drive that will keep building throughout the book? Or is this character at least resisting something? If he or she wants nothing, or is not being threatened or thwarted, you'll have a weak story.

7.   Is there strong conflict to build interest? If there is no trouble, no opposition, you have no story.

8.   Is your main character likable or hateable? A single word can give an effect you never intended. Readers of popular fiction want main characters they can care about—though sometimes it is equally satisfying to watch someone you dislike get his (or her) comeuppance.

9.   Is a minor character steering the story in a wrong direction? Side roads can intrigue a writer, but if they go nowhere, they'd better come out. In fact, this is the final test for any scene, any character, any ingredient of your story: If it can be dropped out and never missed, then it doesn't belong in the first place. A sound plot is like a Chinese puzzle—you can't leave anything out or the whole will collapse. A poorly plotted novel is like a freight train. Take out a car or two and the train will go right on running. If you can do that in a story, something is wrong.

10.   Consider your theme, the point you want to

make: Are you preaching and lecturing the reader? Have you made some sort of statement through your characters and story action without getting up on a soapbox? The author's voice is no longer heard in most of today's fiction. It's there, but it remains behind the scenes.

11. If the gloom never ends, if threats are carried out too consistently, and there is no touch of hope to hold the reader, he will become discouraged and put the book aside. The dangling of hope is the carrot to pull him along. So ask yourself if the setbacks are interlaced with hope.

12. What about logic? What about the motivation of your characters? Here it is very easy to deceive ourselves. We know that it's necessary to reach a certain point, and sometimes we bend our characters unnaturally to achieve this purpose. I call this "author's logic." Often it is illogical and impossible. If you examine the real motivations of your characters, you may need to figure out some other way to reach your goal. If you push your characters *out of character,* the reader will be annoyed.

13. In writing a mystery or suspense novel, it is especially important to pick up every loose end you've dangled and explain it logically. Readers hate loose ends. In your final reading, list such red herrings or question marks, so that you won't forget to clear them up before the end. Yet such explanation must never wind up in undramatic stretches of solid exposition.

14. The first time around you can set everything down as roughly as you like. Polish can come later— the hard part is getting it down. In revising, you will need to look at every word through a magnifying

glass, watching for repetitions, for awkward phrasing (my favorite offense), for the wrong word that will give the wrong effect. And at this stage you will cut out the superfluous words as well.

15. Have you tried for variety in every part of your story? Variety in characters, of course, and in your action, your scenes. Variety also in the words you use, the length and arrangement of sentences and paragraphs. If you begin most of your sentences with a pronoun, a name, a subject, your writing will become monotonous. Rearrange these phrases.

In the end, it is the attention to hundreds of details that adds up to a successful novel. Don't try to be critical of yourself while you write. Forget the "rules." Lose yourself in the story, and let it flow. During revision you must become the critic. In the first writing, you give your story life. In the second, you get it right.

15

GETTING YOUR NOVEL PUBLISHED

While you are writing your novel, your only goal is to finish it. Then, what do you *do* with it?

If you were wise, you probably had a market in mind all along. That is, you were writing in a certain category: mystery, romance, suspense, science fiction, historical, mainstream novel, or whatever terms are being used at the time. It's easier to sell what you've written if it fits into a pigeonhole that can be labeled (no matter how much you dislike pigeonholes). Don't ignore this reality if you are a beginning writer who wants to be published. It's all very well to consider yourself an artist who is above such things, but that is rather unrealistic if you want to sell your book.

If you are not yet sure of an intended market, you can go to the library or bookstore and write down the names and addresses of publishers who seem to be bringing out your type of novel.

In my younger days, we just wrapped up our manuscripts and sent them off—of course, with enclosed postage for return. Today, unfortunately, many publishers will not read manuscripts that come to them "over the transom," but require a query with synopsis, outline, and sample chapters. A "synopsis" is a brief statement about the novel, while an "outline" is more detailed. Personally, I hate to do an outline for anyone except myself to read, but since this must be done these days when you're breaking in, try to make your outline interesting, and don't put everything in. The idea is to make an editor ask for more. Of course, do your best with that first chapter. If your story isn't going to get going until later on, you're in trouble.

If you have submitted an outline to an editor and have been encouraged to go ahead with writing your novel, don't worry when the final version doesn't follow the outline faithfully. No editor will object to improvements in your finished novel. After all, how can any of us know what we're going to write until we write it?

Make your query letter short, stating any qualifications you may have for writing this particular book, and mentioning any previous publications, however modest. If you have no previous credits, merely state that you are submitting a synopsis, etc., with a sample chapter. Although it is now possible to obtain a copyright for your novel manuscript, it is not an advisable procedure. Editors usually want uncopyrighted material, and when the time comes they will take care of registering the copyright. Your contract should state that the copyright be registered in *your* name. Also don't demand terms when you submit your manuscript. You are only trying to get read, and it's very unlikely that anyone will steal your idea.

Presumably, you have subscribed to a good writers' magazine and are aware of the many market lists that are published. These lists include names and addresses of publishers, names of editors (it is important to address your query or manuscript to an editor by name), type of material wanted, length, payment, and whether the publisher will read unsolicited manuscripts.

If you feel that your book stands a good chance, start with hardcover publishers and send it out a few times —only to one publisher at a time. After a half-dozen or so rejections you can then try the softcover market. Since the market for paperback originals has become very large, you may submit your novel to these publishers without trying for hardcover publication. There is more prestige in hardcover publication, though not necessarily more money. In fact, for the successful writer, the big earnings are in the paperback field, and in the book clubs. The latter, however, are usually interested in established "names." If your novel is published first and does well in hardcover, it is likely to be reprinted in paperback. Most first novels sell very modestly, and if you have to earn your living, you'd better have another job to lean on for a while.

The best agents handle the most successful writers, and it's as difficult to be accepted by a top agent as it is to get published at all. There are lesser agents, however, who may be willing to handle your work and give you the attention you need. If you feel more comfortable with someone to intercede for you, they may be able to get your manuscript read more easily.

Agents generally get a ten percent commission, and sometimes fifteen or even twenty percent, on your earnings from royalties (the higher percentages are becoming more common). For sales of foreign rights, the commissions vary. Look up *Literary Market Place* (Bowker) in your library or consult *The Writer's Handbook* (The Writer, Inc.) for names and addresses of literary agents. Don't send your manuscript in cold.

Introductions to publishers or agents by a writer, or someone known to them, are always helpful, though in the beginning they may be hard to come by. I had none when I sold my first book. An introduction can get you a hearing, at least, though it will not sell your manuscript unless it is good.

The most important rule through all this painful time is not to let the rejections discourage you. (You should be working on something else by this time, anyway.) Remember—a manuscript sitting on a shelf isn't going to sell. Somewhere along the way, by sending it out, you may find a few enlightening words written on the rejection slip—which means that someone is watching, and you should try again.

Eventually, if you are persistent, if you keep writing, you *will* find a publisher, and the august figure of an editor will come into your life. There are all kinds of editors. Some you will like and some you won't, but in the beginning it's wise to listen and try to learn from anyone who is willing to work with you. This is not the time to be independent. Having an agent won't change very much until you have earned the right to a better deal. Agents can explain a contract—and that helps. When you have a real business to handle, then you will need a good agent to look out for your interests, retain certain rights for you, sell your work abroad, or to the movies and television. None of this is easy.

Here's my picture of an ideal editor: Interested in *me* and my writing. Ready to help me grow as a writer. Willing to listen. One who believes I can do it and will offer encouragement when I'm discouraged. I want an editor who is my friend, and I am apt to forget that all editors have a whole stable of writing "friends." Writers tend to wail and beat their breasts despairingly at the slightest criticism. Editors need patience. Writers are highly subjective individuals; the best editors are objective. This makes a good combination, when it happens.

Unfortunately, not all editors are good critics—they have other things to do. So when you find one who is, you're lucky. Hold on.

The editor-writer relationship can generate considerable emotion. We writers need to be believed in, to be praised for what we do right, to be told tactfully what is wrong, and encouraged to go ahead and make it better. Emerson said it very well: "Our chief want in life is someone to make us do what we can." Most of us could do a great deal more than we believe we can, so that a critic whom we can trust, and who has confidence in our ability, is sure to become a valued and much loved friend. That's the way writers are!

———

This is a book about *writing*. I hope it's a book that you will mark up and use—as I do my collected books on writing. I hope as well that you've found in it some of the encouragement we all need to keep us going. I have been where you are, and you will be where I am (published)—if you never give up.

Whatever sort of writing you do, don't let anyone put you down. The literary top is for the few, and there is room all the way up. Above all, keep an eye on those readers out there and remember the value of what we have to give them. We are entertainers first, but as entertainers we may also have much more to offer.